EMBERS
of the
ANCIENT FLAME

EMBERS

of the
ANCIENT FLAME
2ND EDITION

LATIN LOVE POETRY SELECTIONS FROM
CATULLUS, HORACE, AND OVID

by
CAROL A. MURPHY
DANIEL G. THIEM
RYAN T. MOORE

Bolchazy-Carducci Publishers, Inc.
Wauconda, Illinois USA

General Editor:
Laurie Haight Keenan

Contributing Editor:
Andrew J. Adams

Cover Design & Typography:
Adam Phillip Velez

Embers of the Ancient Flame, 2nd Edition

by Carol A. Murphy, Daniel G. Thiem, Ryan T. Moore

Bolchazy-Carducci Publishers, Inc.
1000 Brown Street
Wauconda, IL 60084 USA
www.bolchazy.com

Printed in the United States of America
2005
by Publishers Graphics

ISBN-13: 978-0-86516-609-7
ISBN-10: 0-86516-609-9

Library of Congress Cataloging-in-Publication Data

Embers of the ancient flame : Latin love poetry selections from Catullus, Horace, and
Ovid / [edited] by Carol A. Murphy, Daniel G. Thiem, Ryan T. Moore.-- 2nd ed.
    p. cm.
Poems in Latin; commentaries in English.
Includes bibliographical references (p.   ).
ISBN-13: 978-0-86516-609-7
ISBN-10: 0-86516-609-9 (pbk. : alk. paper)
1. Love poetry, Latin. 2. Latin language--Readers. I. Murphy, Carol A., 1944- II.
Thiem, Daniel G., 1977- III. Moore, Ryan T., 1977- IV. Title.

PA6135.L68E43 2005
871'.010803543--dc22

2005009242

ULTIMAE CLASSI IB/AP
GRATIAS VOBIS

Nathaniel
Lauren
Ilya
Shelby
Brian
Ryan
Yi Ting

CONTENTS

PREFACE
TO THE SECOND EDITION

This text was created as an introduction to the love poetry of three remarkable Latin poets. The selections were chosen to accommodate the Love Poetry topic selection in the Upper and Standard Level Syllabus of the International Baccalaureate Program, and includes only those poems included in the syllabus. Devotees of Catullus may bemoan the absence of several Catullan standards, such as 11 and 101, but the committee was adamant about the number of lines for which students are held responsible on the exam. It is assumed, moreover, that the teacher will supplement the syllabus with any pieces of literature which he or she deems appropriate to their students' learning experience. We have included a brief introduction to poetic meter, some historical background, maps and an abbreviated glossary. We have added a parallel gloss as an aid for student translation, with such notes as we felt appropriate for comprehension of the poem at hand. The student is encouraged to consult one of the commentaries or other texts suggested in the Reading List for more in-depth information on the authors, historical period, Latin poetic meter, or other peculiarities of the genre. In addition, it is assumed that each student has access to a good dictionary for words not included in the text. In as much as Paper I of the International Baccalaureate Exam requires the student to translate an unseen passage with a dictionary, we felt it would be a disservice to the student to gloss every word or point out each figure of speech.

The Latin texts are taken from the *Scriptorum Classicorum Bibliotheca Oxoniensis,* Oxford University Press.

MAPS

ITALY

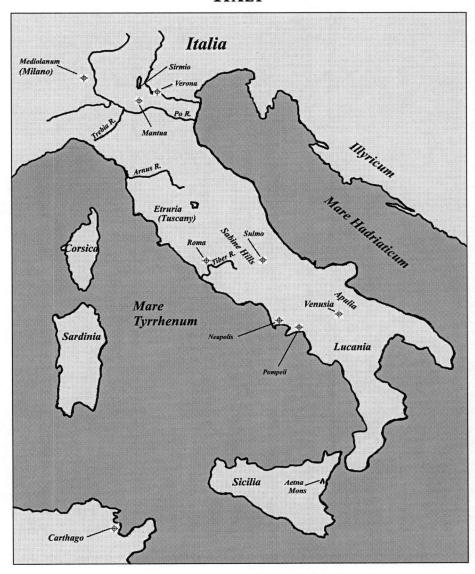

The Mediterranean

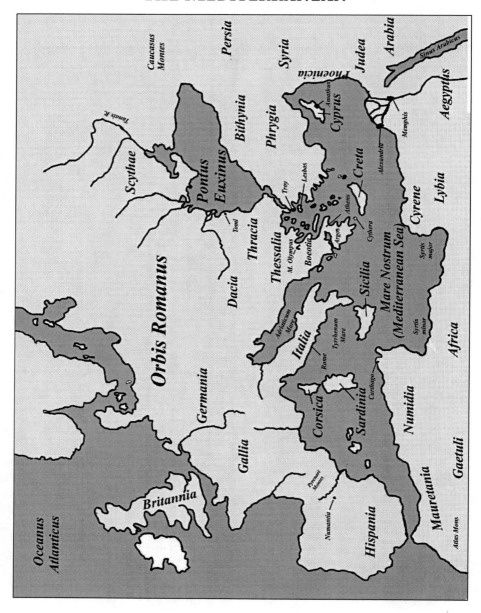

A NOTE TO THE STUDENT

A Brief Introduction to Reading
Catullus, Horace, and Ovid

We examine the history of Rome because it is a mosaic of human expression and experience. Poetry, architecture, sculpture, government, and society were all viable elements which formed the world of Rome. These expressions of the human condition provide insight and fascinating detail about those men and women of antiquity—their lives, their attitudes on freedom, slavery, government, money, and territorial expansion—reactions which are remarkably similar to our own historical perspectives. We study Rome because it is, in many ways, a distant echo of our lives today.

There is no more common period studied in Roman history than that of Julius Caesar and the emperor Augustus. Political turbulence and social changes marked this era as one of the most influential and defining times in the history of Western civilization. Whether we examine the continuing civil wars, prominence of wealth among an elite few, an ill-defined policy of expansion, exploitation and gold-lust, or any number of social practices, we invariably discover either a subtle hint or a blinding parallel with life in the modern Western world. Yet, without literature, art, government, and history, we would know precious little about these fascinating aspects of Roman daily life.

Fortunately, however, there exists a vast corpus of material collected over time that can provide windows into life in ancient Rome. Perhaps the most lucid and personal window into Roman life is through her poetry. Roman poetry is a collection of commentaries on contemporary Roman life, and a reflection of a refined literary tradition founded on continuous creativity and clever importation. From such established Greek masters as Sappho and Callimachus, Roman poets borrowed meters and literary traditions as well as the didactic and epic voices of Hesiod and Homer. They subsequently blended those traditions with new, Roman alterations to comment upon their own lives and times.

The lives and times of Catullus, Horace, and Ovid were bustling with civil war and political upheaval that saw the fall of Republican government and the rise of the Principate. Everything from changing social status to civil strife influenced these poets and their literature. Political allegiance and commentary, in addition to patronage with such men as Maecenas, are common themes in Horace and Ovid; whereas, aristocratic longing and uncertainty combined with a turbulent love life to form Catullus' work. Overlaying these poems is a tense longing for peace and stability that had been remarkably absent in the lives of each of these men. Catullus would never see the rise of Augustus and a lasting peace *(Pax Romana),* but Ovid and Horace certainly did, and the flowing, decidedly leisurely tone to their poetry reflects this fact well. Catullus, while remarkably fresh and human, is nonetheless constantly plagued by feelings of guilt and insecurity for his own leisurely exploits with poetry, which the late Republican aristocracy neither tolerated nor preferred.

As you read the works of Catullus, Horace and Ovid, examine them not as a grand translation puzzle awaiting a solution, but as literature, unrolling the centuries-old stories of deception, love, fear, hate, innocence, lust, honor, betrayal, and beauty. This was Rome!

CATULLUS

Bridal toilette, Villa of the Mysteries, Pompeii.
Photograph by Raymond V. Schroder, S. J.

CATULLUS

Gaius Valerius Catullus, as he is named by literary tradition, was probably born in Verona in about 84 BC, although some sources make that 87. His family was obviously wealthy, since they possessed villas in Sirmio (in the north) and Tivoli. His family's status is further confirmed by the fact that he had a social relationship with Julius Caesar and with the consul (or at least the consul's wife) Q. Metellus Celer, in about 60 BC. General literary commentary assumes that the "Lesbia" in Catullus' poems was Clodia, sister of P. Clodius Pulcher. Clodius was the enemy of Cicero and the center of much political and social comment of the period, as was his sister. A problem with this acknowledgement of Clodia as Lesbia lies in the fact that Clodia had two sisters, so either of them might be possibilities. We know from his own writings that he was in Bithynia, serving in the military under the leadership of Memmius, from 57 to 56 BC Jerome (Chronica) gives the death date of Catullus as 54. He was thirty then, according to Jerome's chronology, which made him a very young man during his entire creative career. That it was a brief career is widely accepted and lamented, and the cause of death is unknown; although since the nature of much of his poetry was very inflammatory and actually libelous by modern standards, one could reliably speculate that he disappeared under mysterious circumstances.

CATULLUS 2, 2B: NOTES

Meter: Hendecasyllabics

This poem is commonly called "The Sparrow," since in its entirety it is a poetic APOSTROPHE to a "passer," a small bird, possibly a blue thrush. Since among the classical community there is some discussion about the nature and function of this "passer," the student is encouraged to read and make an independent decision. Catullus, ever the tortured lover, implies that this small "bird" is allowed an intimacy with Lesbia which Catullus himself is denied. Is the bird avian, inanimate, or human? Whichever one chooses, the IRONY is inescapable.

1. **passer, passeris,** *m.,* sparrow

2. **quicum = quocum (cum quo)**

   sinu: *from* **sinus, -us,** *m.,* curve, fold, bosom, lap, pocket

3. **primum digitum:** literally, "foremost finger," but its meaning is really idiomatic for "finger-tip"

   appetenti: *pres. part. from* **appeto,** 3, seek, attack, try to reach

4. **solet:** requires a complementary infinitive. In this case, Catullus places the main verb (**solet**) at the end of a series of complimentary infinitives.

   morsus, -us, *m.,* bite

5. **nitenti:** *pres. part. from* **niteo,** 2, shine, glitter, be sleek and plump; *either dat. or abl., depending upon one's interpretation.*

6. **nescio quid:** sometimes written as one word; read with **carum** as acc. of specification: "to make I don't know what dear joke."

   lubet = libet: impersonal verb + infinitive (**iocari**)

7. **solaciolum:** *dim. of* **solacium, -i,** *n.,* solace or comfort

8. **acquiescat: acquiesco (adquiesco),** 3, assent, subside, lie down to rest

   ardor, ardoris, *m.,* passion, fire, intensity, brightness

9. **sicut,** *adv.,* just as, as it were

10. **levare:** lift, relieve, lessen

Meter: Hendecasyllabics

This poem is a fragment of some larger work. The labeling conventions of literary classification place it here, since some scholars felt it may be a part of Poem 2, although it is not fundamentally linked to the preceding poem. The reference is to Atalanta, a woman from Greek mythology who vowed to marry any suitor who could defeat her in a foot race. Many tried and failed, but Hippomenes, at the suggestion of Venus, devised a clever plan: he threw three golden apples along the race course which the curious Atalanta stopped to collect during the race. The brief interlude gave him the chance he needed to gain the lead in the contest, and to defeat Atalanta, thus claiming her as his bride. The implication inherent in the story is that this loss was not odious to Atalanta.

2. **pernici: pernix, pernicis:** *adj.,* agile, fleet of foot

3. **zonam: zona, -ae,** *f.,* a woman's girdle or belt

   soluit: solvo, 3, loosen, untie, cast off

The reference to the loosening of a woman's belt is an allusion to lost virginity.

ligatam: *p.p. of* **ligo,** 1, tied together, bound up

CATULLUS 2

Passer, deliciae meae puellae,
quicum ludere, quem in sinu tenere,
cui primum digitum dare appetenti
et acris solet incitare morsus,
cum desiderio meo nitenti   5
carum nescio quid lubet iocari,
et solaciolum sui doloris,
credo, ut tum gravis acquiescat ardor:
tecum ludere sicut ipsa possem
et tristis animi levare curas!   10

CATULLUS 2B

tam gratum est mihi quam ferunt puellae
pernici aureolum fuisse malum,
quod zonam soluit diu ligatam.

CATULLUS 5: NOTES

Meter: Hendecasyllabics

This poem has a companion in Horace's *Ode* 1.11 (*carpe diem*) and a theme much adored by poets of all time periods: Let us live and love with no regard to what people say; for life is short and when it is over, death is eternal and unsuited to passion. Catullus introduces a common theme that is prevalent throughout his poetry, the idea of creating a persona. The role that Lesbia plays in Catullus' poetry is symbolic and representative of a personality with whom Catullus' audience can identify. The student of Catullus must examine the poetry and its characters from both the perspective of its historical significance within the political and social tide of the time, and from the humanistic representations that the characters fulfill.

There is some argument, mostly due to a lack of complete textual or historical evidence, concerning the identity of Lesbia. Her name, according to Apuleius, is largely agreed to be a pseudonym for Clodia, the sister of P. Clodius Pulcher, a man known for scandal, sacrilege, and for his enmity toward Cicero. If she was, in fact, the wife of Quintus Metellus Celer, consul in 60 BC, interesting political and social conclusions can be drawn. Clodia, widely known for her affair with Caelius and eventual role in Cicero's famous defense of the same (*Pro Caelio*), is thought to have led a somewhat devious and suspect life, frequenting the company of young men.

1. **vivamus...amemus:** hortatory subjunctives

   Notice the focus gained by the author's placement of **mea Lesbia**. These words capture the central theme of the poem, and, some argue, of his poetry in general: the poem and his mind always center on Lesbia. She is between "live" and "love."

2. **senum:** senex, senis, *m.*, old man

   severiorum: *comp. of* **severus** *adj.*, strict, severe, forbidding. The use of this adjective hints at the social rift growing between the artfully inspired young aristocrats, such as Catullus, and the older, more established cadre of the republic's current leaders, such as M. Tullius Cicero, C. Julius Caesar, et al.

3. **unius:** *gen. of* **unus, -a, -um,** *adj.;* scan the *i* short

   assis: as, assis, *m.,* a unit of money, comparable to a penny. Genitive of value with **aestimemus**

4. **soles:** *from* **sol, solis,** *m.,* sun

   occidere: here, "sunset" with **redire,** *comp. infinitive with* **possunt:** "suns (are able to) set and return."

5. **semel,** *adv.,* once, once and for all, the first time

6. **dormienda:** passive periphrastic

7. **basia:** basium, -i, *n.,* kiss

   mi = mihi

7–10: **deinde** and **dein** are used to accommodate metrical necessities in the poem. The ANAPHORAS created in lines 7–10 add to the **conturbabimus** in 11.

11. **conturbo,** 1, upset or disquiet; throw into disorder (particularly in regard to financial matters, as the word is often used by Cicero). The use of this verb hints at a deliberate act of deception by Catullus and Lesbia. It is used in the poem not in the sense of "keeping quiet about," but more for the purpose of "stirring things up" with their kisses.

12. **invidere:** look inward; hence, look upon with 'an evil eye' or be envious of

13. **sciat:** *subjunctive of* **scio,** 4, know

Catullus 5

Vivamus, mea Lesbia, atque amemus,
rumoresque senum severiorum
omnes unius aestimemus assis!
soles occidere et redire possunt:
nobis cum semel occidit brevis lux,   5
nox est perpetua una dormienda.
da mi basia mille, deinde centum,
dein mille altera, dein secunda centum,
deinde usque altera mille, deinde centum.
dein, cum milia multa fecerimus,   10
conturbabimus illa, ne sciamus,
aut ne quis malus invidere possit,
cum tantum sciat esse basiorum.

CATULLUS 7: NOTES

Meter: Hendecasyllabics

In this poem, Catullus includes an intriguing catalogue of foreign names and places. As an aristocrat in general, and a provincial aristocrat especially, Catullus and his contemporaries would have frequented the provinces as part of their cultural and professional training. Travel and business in provincial cities and ports often established networks of resources into which an aspiring lawyer or politician could tap in critical situations or for simple favors.

1. **quaeris: quaero,** 3, search for or inquire into

2. **sint:** subjunctive of *esse*

   superque: and more, and a surfeit

3. **Libyssae: Libyssus, -a, -um,** *adj.,* Libyan, from Libya

   harenae: harena, -ae, *f.,* sand; beach, shore

4. **lasarpiciferis, -e,** *adj.,* producing asafoetida, or silphium; silphium is a plant native to the northern tier of Africa, especially in the province of Cyrene, where the plant was not only wild, but also abundantly fruitful for the local export economy. Silphium was the birth-control plant of antiquity, and was in such demand that it was harvested to extinction by the third century AD.

   Cyrenis: Cyrene, -is, *f.,* a town and province in northern Africa. It was founded by the Greeks under peaceful overtones with the neighboring Libyans and Egyptians, but was eventually threatened by the same people. Once a steady influx of Greek colonists began to overcrowd and expand into the surrounding area, there began border skirmishes and acts of war. Egyptians and Libyans were too weak for the Greeks, but the Romans soon overpowered all of them and made it their own.

5. **oraclum = oraculum:** The oracle to Zeus Ammon (Juppiter Hammon) was consulted even by Alexander the Great.

   aestuosi: aestuosus, -a, -um, *adj.,* hot, steamy. In this case there is a double reference to the intense heat of Saharan Africa and to Zeus Ammon, whose image appeared on coins of Cyrene, thus making it a TRANSFERRED EPITHET.

6. **Batti: Battus, -i,** *m.,* the given name of Aristotle of Thera, the founder of Cyrene.

7. **sidera: sidus, sideris,** *n.,* star

10. **vesano: vesanus, -a, -um,** *adj.,* mad, wild

    The CHIASMUS in 10 almost suggests that mad Catullus "consumes" enough and more of her kisses.

11. **quae:** antecedent is **multa basia.**

    pernumerare, 1, enumerate, count out, tally

12. **fascinare,** 1, curse, put a spell upon, bewitch

    These last two lines return us to Poem 5, where the "old men" were attempting to keep a tally of illicit kisses (according to Catullus).

Catullus 7

Quaeris, quot mihi basiationes
tuae, Lesbia, sint satis superque.
quam magnus numerus Libyssae harenae
lasarpiciferis iacet Cyrenis
oraclum Iovis inter aestuosi   5
et Batti veteris sacrum sepulcrum;
aut quam sidera multa, cum tacet nox,
furtivos hominum vident amores:
tam te basia multa basiare
vesano satis et super Catullo est,   10
quae nec pernumerare curiosi
possint nec mala fascinare lingua.

CATULLUS 8: NOTES

Meter: Limping Iambics

In the first two words of this poem, we discover that the poet is talking to himself; obviously, given that the foremost word is "miser," we know that he is also feeling very sorry for himself. He proceeds to list the facts, and then to give himself sound advice. He then turns his attention to the "puella" and proceeds with a litany of rhetorical questions which compare to a similar chastisement in Horace, *Ode* 1.25. In the last line, he addresses himself again, obviously confirmed in his resolve.

1. **desinas: desino,** 3, cease, desist; iussive subjunctive

    ineptire: ineptio, 4, act silly, to demonstrate foolish behavior

2. **ducas: duco,** 3, think or consider; it governs the indirect statement of which **perditum** (*esse*) is the verb and **quod** (*vides perisse*) the subject.

    perisse: *from* **pereo,** 4, vanish, perish

    perditum: perdo, 3, lose, ruin

3. **fulsere: fulgeo,** 2, flash, shine; 3rd pl. perf.

4. **ventitabas: ventito,** 1, come frequently or habitually

5. **nobis:** plural for the singular Catullus.

    The rest of this line is an echo of Poem 87.

6. **fiebant: fio,** 4, be made or become

7. **nec...nolebat:** LITOTES

8. Compare with 3.

9. **nunc...non...noli:** the negatives include the vocative: **impotens**

10. **sectare: sector,** 1, follow (dep. imperative)

11. **obstinata: obstinatus, -a, -um,** *adj.,* steady, firm

    obdura: obduro, 1, persist, endure

13. **requiret: requiro,** 3, seek, ask about

    Note the **nec...nec** here echoes 10.

14. **nulla:** *abl. from* **nullus, a, um:** colloquial emphatic, none, not any

15. **vae:** *interj.,* Woe to you!

16. **adibit: adeo, -ire, -ii (-ivi), -itus,** 4, go forth, go out with

17. **cuius esse diceris:** Figuratively, "To whom will you belong?" Literally, "Whose will you be said to be?"

18. **mordebis: mordeo,** 2, bite

19. **destinatus: destino,** 1, determine

    Compare the final injunction from the poet to himself with the opening line.

CATULLUS 8

Miser Catulle, desinas ineptire,
et quod vides perisse perditum ducas.
fulsere quondam candidi tibi soles,
cum ventitabas quo puella ducebat
amata nobis quantum amabitur nulla.   5
ibi illa multa cum iocosa fiebant,
quae tu volebas nec puella nolebat,
fulsere vere candidi tibi soles.
nunc iam illa non volt: tu quoque impotens noli,
nec quae fugit sectare, nec miser vive,   10
sed obstinata mente perfer, obdura.
vale, puella. iam Catullus obdurat,
nec te requiret nec rogabit invitam.
at tu dolebis, cum rogaberis nulla.
scelesta, vae te, quae tibi manet vita?   15
quis nunc te adibit? cui videberis bella?
quem nunc amabis? cuius esse diceris?
quem basiabis? cui labella mordebis?
at tu, Catulle, destinatus obdura.

Catullus 45: Notes

Meter: Hendecasyllabics

This is a poem about a Roman boy who is very much in love with a Greek girl. It is highly unlikely, at this period of time, that this girl was of his station, particularly given his name. The poet paints us a charming picture of mutual love and adoration, fully condoning (as does Venus) their dissimilar social strata. Compare this poem with *Ode* 2.4 by Horace, where he consoles his friend and encourages him not to abandon his love for his serving maid.

1. **Acmen:** Greek acc. The word means "prime, flower," and in some cases, "the prime of a man's life," which is appropriate in the context of this poem.

   Septimius: Not an unusual, although not a common name for a Roman man: it is a *gentilicium* (one referring to a specific clan). The value of its use perhaps is not in its peculiarity, but its distinctly Roman nature.

2. **gremio:** gremium, -i, *n.*, lap

3. **ni:** to complete the conditional clause which this introduces, look to **veniam** in 7.

   perdite, *adv.,* desperately

   porro, *adv.,* hereafter, further, in future. Note the ALLITERATION

4. **assidue,** *adv.,* continually, constantly. Note how this line is framed: **omnes annos** at the ends, framing **sum paratus** with the central thought being **assidue.**

5. **pote:** *from* **potest;** *supply* **"is qui potest..."**

6. **tosta:** torreo, 2, be parched, dried-up

7. **caesio:** caesius, -a, -um, *adj.,* blue-grey in color (especially of the eyes)

   obvius, -a, -um, *adj. + dat.,* in the way of, across from

9. **sternuit:** sternuo, 3, sneeze. It was considered good luck, among Romans, when someone sneezed on the left; Greeks had the same superstition, but the sneeze needed to be on the right. Here, since Love sneezes in both directions, the omens are good for both Acme and Septimius.

11. **ebrios:** ebrius, -a, -um, *adj.,* drunk or intoxicated

    ocellos: ocellus, -i, *adj.,* little eyes (dim. of oculus)

12. **suaviata,** *p.p.:* **suavior,** *dep.,* kiss

13. **Septimille,** *voc.,* a diminutive term of endearment for Septimius

14–16. Acme's speech flows as softly as her kisses with the ALLITERATION of *m*'s, ending with the use of *medullis,* the marrow or innermost part which was considered the seat of emotion, more complex and tempered than ordinary feeling.

19. **auspicio:** auspicium, -i, *n.* (auspex), discovering the will of the gods by observing the flights of birds; *hence,* omen or sign

20. Note the ALLITERATION with the letter *a* in this line and the several preceding lines

    The ASSONANCE of the "ah, ah, ah..." has a pleasing, approving sound.

22. **Syrias Britanniasque:** These provinces are at opposite ends of the Empire and are mentioned here for that specific reason. They are far removed from the Roman world that Septimius knows, yet he prefers his Acme to all the unknown delights he might find in exotic places.

24. **libidines:** libido, libidinis, *f.,* desire

    delicias libidinesque: HENDIADYS

25. **beatiores:** *comp. of* **beatus, -a, -um,** *adj.,* more blessed

Catullus 45

Acmen Septimius suos amores
tenens in gremio "mea" inquit "Acme,
ni te perdite amo atque amare porro
omnes sum assidue paratus annos,
quantum qui pote plurimum perire,   5
solus in Libya Indiaque tosta
caesio veniam obvius leoni."
hoc ut dixit, Amor sinistra ut ante
dextra sternuit approbationem.
      at Acme leviter caput reflectens   10
et dulcis pueri ebrios ocellos
illo purpureo ore suaviata,
"sic," inquit "mea vita Septimille,
huic uni domino usque serviamus,
ut multo mihi maior acriorque   15
ignis mollibus ardet in medullis."
hoc ut dixit, Amor sinistra ut ante
dextra sternuit approbationem.
      nunc ab auspicio bono profecti
mutuis animis amant amantur.   20
unam Septimius misellus Acmen
mavult quam Syrias Britanniasque:
uno in Septimio fidelis Acme
facit delicias libidinesque.
quis ullos homines beatiores   25
vidit, quis Venerem auspicatiorem?

CATULLUS 51: NOTES

Meter: Sapphic Strophe

This poem follows the model of a Greek original composed by Sappho, a translation of which is included below. Catullus 11 and 51, are the only poems in the author's extant collection which utilize the Sapphic Strophe. Some scholars have argued that 11 and 51 are the first and last poems addressed to Lesbia. Their respective subject matter seems to support this theory. Catullus seems to have been a great admirer of Sappho, as would be indicated by his use of "Lesbia" as a pseudonym for his lady. Sappho was a native of the island of Lesbos in the Aegean Sea. Whether or not Lesbia represents a real person from Catullus' life is almost inconsequential. From a fictional perspective, his use of Sapphic meter and his reference to "Lesbia" is an illuminating glance into the mind of Catullus.

The first stanza opens with a somewhat bold declaration that the man sitting across from Lesbia seems equal—or superior to—a god (*Deo*). Catullus, covering his overt impiety, quickly adds *si fas est*. Catullus looks on, speechless and powerless to act; and so he would be, in fact, if the man in question *were* one of the gods, seducing his Lesbia, as gods were free to seduce mortals. Toward the end of the piece, Catullus almost shakes himself free of the spell and advises himself that he obviously has too much time on his hands, a condition which has brought down more powerful men than himself.

1. **par: par, paris,** *adj.* or *noun,* equal to

2. **divos: divus, -i,** *m.,* god

3. **adversus,** *adv.* or *prep. + acc.,* opposite

   Note that the first word in lines 1, 2, & 3 refers to "that man."

7. **super,** *adv.,* remains, is in addition to, can be added

8. This line is not in the Oxford text, but is usually added for clarity, as well as to create more of a parallel with Sappho's poem 31 (below), citing either the Doering or the Ritter restoration (see Lee, Garrison, F. W. Cornish, G. P. Goold, et al.).

9. **torpet: torpeo,** 2, be numb, be struck incapable of motion

   tenuis, -e, *adj.,* thin, faint, weak

10. **demanat: demano,** 1, run or drip down.

    The enclitic *-pte* is emphatic. Notice what is happening with the sound in this fourth stanza (9–12) the ASSONANCE and ALLITERATION are intensified by the ONOMATOPOEIA in **tintinant** and the METONYMY in **lumina.**

13. **otium, -i,** *n.,* leisure. Note the parallel structure of the last three lines and the first; here the repeated word is *otium.*

14. **gestis: gestio, -ire,** 4, desire eagerly, exult

Sappho 31

To me he seems equal to the gods,
the man who sits opposite you
and hears your sweet voice nearby

and longed-for laughter; this makes
my heart flutter in my chest.
For when I see you, <Brokhea>, then
there is no voice in me,

but my tongue shatters, a delicate
fire soon burns under my skin,
nothing is seen by my eyes, buzzing
in my ears,

sweat pours over me, wild
trembling everywhere; I turn green as grass,
and I seem to be not far from death.
But...

<all must be dared....>

Translated by Ryan T. Moore

Catullus 51

Ille mi par esse deo videtur,
ille, si fas est, superare divos,
qui sedens adversus identidem te
    spectat et audit

dulce ridentem, misero quod omnis   5
eripit sensus mihi: nam simul te,
Lesbia, aspexi, nihil est super mi
    <vocis in ore>

lingua sed torpet, tenuis sub artus
flamma demanat, sonitu suopte   10
tintinant aures, gemina teguntur
    lumina nocte.

otium, Catulle, tibi molestum est:
otio exsultas nimiumque gestis:
otium et reges prius et beatas   15
    perdidit urbes.

CATULLUS 62: NOTES

Meter: Dactylic Hexameter

This poem was probably a commissioned piece, one requested of Catullus. In it, he employs a standard Hymn to Hymen, the wedding god. This is a Latin adaptation of the Greek god's name. The elongated version of the word, *Hymenaee*, is a quantitative variation used as both a metrical filler and emphatic addition. Roman and Greek wedding customs are exhibited here. The feast in this poem is Greek in origin, and its use here moves the scene from Rome to Greece. Knowledge of Greek custom and belief was a characteristic, if not requirement, of the Roman aristocracy. From the opening words *Vesper adest* we get the sense of anticipation which takes us through the entire poem.

In keeping with custom, women and men did not eat at the same table at Greek weddings. Instead, they sat opposite from one another during the feast, and as we now discover, challenged each other in song competition. This type of poem, where males respond to the females in song, is called *amoebean*.

1. *The young men begin.*

    consurgite: consurgo, 3, rise together

3. **tempus:** supply *est*

    linquere: linquo, 3, leave or depart from

5. Like any other song, this is the chorus, repeated at the end of each stanza.

6. *The young women respond.*

    cernitis: cerno, 3, perceive

    contra, *adv.,* opposite, on the opposite side

7. **nimirum,** *adv.,* undoubtedly

    Oetaeos: Mt. Oeta south of Mt. Olympus. Notice also the parallel to lines 1–2, where the Vesper lifts the light and Olympus is the mountain. Here, the light is ironically **Noctifer,** "the bearer of night," more pointedly the precursor to night. Both sequences clearly suggest an evening marriage festival from two distinct points of view.

8. **certest:** colloquial *certe est,* with **sic** it has the meaning "yes, that's certain"

    viden = videsne: The enclitic **-ne** is syncopated into the word in order to form a two-syllable version of **videsne,** similar to **mi** for **mihi,** or to compare in this same line, **exsiluere** for **exsiluerunt.**

    perniciter, *adv.,* swiftly

9. **exsiluere: exsileo,** 4, spring up, jump

    temere, *adv.,* accidentally, by chance; casually

11–15. *The dialogue switches back to the men's table.* The anticipation of competition between the two tables is growing. Each side marvels at the other's ability to perform, and the fortitude of their song. This is a competition to be won and perception of ability is paramount.

11. **palma, -ae,** *f.,* the palm of victory

12. **meditata** (supply *esse*): **meditor, -ari,** *dep.,* practice or rehearse

14. **mirum: mirus, -a, -um,** *adj.,* wonderful, astonishing

15. **divisimus: divido,** 3, divide, separate into parts

16. **iure,** *adv.,* rightly

    curam: care or diligence in practice, as conducted by the women's table.

17. **saltem,** *adv., emphasizes* **nunc:** at least, at all events

20. *The song begins now as the young women sing an* APOSTROPHE *to Hesperus, the evening star* (Greek name).

21. **avellere: avello,** 3, tear away. Note the parallels in lines 21 and 22, the duplication of **complexu, avellere, natam** and **matris.** This is a reference to the marriage custom of the groom "ripping" his bride from the arms of her mother, reminiscent of the rape of the Sabines at the time of Romulus.

23. **castam: castus, -a, -um,** *adj.,* pure, chaste

24. **capta urbe:** The inference being made by the women is that the young wife is treated in the same way that soldiers treat women captured in an enemy city.

CATULLUS 62

Vesper adest, iuvenes, consurgite: Vesper Olympo
exspectata diu vix tandem lumina tollit.
surgere iam tempus, iam pinguis linquere mensas,
iam veniet virgo, iam dicetur hymenaeus.
Hymen o Hymenaee, Hymen ades o Hymenaee!　　　　5

Cernitis, innuptae, iuvenes? consurgite contra;
nimirum Oetaeos ostendit Noctifer ignes.
sic certest; viden ut perniciter exsiluere?
non temere exsiluere: canent quod vincere par est.
Hymen o Hymenaee, Hymen ades o Hymenaee!　　　　10

Non facilis nobis, aequales, palma parata est;
aspicite, innuptae secum ut meditata requirunt.
non frustra meditantur: habent memorabile quod sit;
nec mirum, penitus quae tota mente laborant.
nos alio mentes, alio divisimus aures;　　　　15
iure igitur vincemur: amat victoria curam.
quare nunc animos saltem convertite vestros;
dicere iam incipient, iam respondere decebit.
Hymen o Hymenaee, Hymen ades o Hymenaee!

Hespere, quis caelo fertur crudelior ignis?　　　　20
qui natam possis complexu avellere matris,
complexu matris retinentem avellere natam,
et iuveni ardenti castam donare puellam.
quid faciunt hostes capta crudelius urbe?
Hymen o Hymenaee, Hymen ades o Hymenaee!　　　　25

26. *The men respond, describing the same scene as the girls, but with the emphasis.* What could be more wonderful, since it was the parents themselves who made the arrangement.

27. **desponsa: despondeo,** 2, pledge or promise, especially in marriage

    firmes: firmo, 1, make firm or strengthen

28. **pepigere: pango,** 3, fix, settle, agree upon

29. **iunxere: iungo,** 3, join, unite (3rd. pl. perf.)

30. **felici: felix, felicis,** *adj.,* lucky, of good omen; fertile, fruitful

    optatius, *comp. adj.,* wished-for, desired

32. *This is the first line of the women's response.* However, it is incomplete; we can only assume that it goes on about the one of them who is being carried off. We can infer that the stanza attempts to deal with men being thieves in the night, perhaps a reference to the wedding night as we can gather from the men's response in the next stanza, which is also partially missing, but readable in lines in 33–37.

34. **latent: lateo,** 2, lie hidden, be concealed or sheltered

    revertens: reverto, 3, turn back, return

35. **Eous:** the morning star, the same one as the evening star, *Vesper.*

36. **ficto:** *p.p.* **fingo,** 3, shape, arrange; hence the participle form means invented, fabricated, "made-up"

37. Idiomatically, "So what if they gather complaints against you, when, in silent thought, they must have you?" The young men are using the age-old disclaimer that in secret all women want to be carried off and ravished.

39. The women introduce this epic SIMILE, which serves two functions in this poem. First, it lends the appearance and weight of an epic poem, consistent with meter and gravity of subject matter. Second, the SIMILE provides an elusive, but lucid foreground in which the *amoebean* contest may continue and ultimately conclude.

    Note the sounds associated with the ALLITERATION of **saeptis secretus:** the *s* continues through **nascitur** and **hortis** as a "sh-h-h-."

    saeptis: saepio, 4, shut in, surround with a hedge, enclose

40. **convolsus: convello,** 3, tear or pull away

    aratro: aratrum, -i, *n.,* the plough

41. Note the ASYNDETON in this line.

    mulcent: mulceo, 2, stroke, touch lightly

42. **optavere:** 3rd pl. perf.

43. **ungui: unguis, -is,** *m.,* a finger or toenail. It carries a meaning which is easy to visualize in the context of the SIMILE, that of a flower being snapped off with a finger nail; further it also carries a more subjective meaning because the term **unguis** was used to show scorn or disapproval.

44. Note the ANTITHESIS created by this line and 42. The effect is somewhat like looking at a mirror image. In this poem, the reflection centers on the idea of a flower being plucked from its stem: once desired, now despised.

45. **dum...dum:** *correlative,* as long as...so long

    suis: *substantive,* to her own (family, friends, etc.)

Hespere, quis caelo lucet iucundior ignis?
qui desponsa tua firmes conubia flamma,
quae pepigere viri, pepigerunt ante parentes,
nec iunxere prius quam se tuus extulit ardor.
quid datur a divis felici optatius hora? 30
Hymen o Hymenaee, Hymen ades o Hymenaee!

Hesperus e nobis, aequales, abstulit unam.
* * * * * * * * * *
namque tuo adventu vigilat custodia semper,
nocte latent fures, quos idem saepe revertens,
Hespere, mutato comprendis nomine Eous. 35
at lubet innuptis ficto te carpere questu.
quid tum, si carpunt, tacita quem mente requirunt?
Hymen o Hymenaee, Hymen ades o Hymenaee!

Ut flos in saeptis secretus nascitur hortis,
ignotus pecori, nullo convolsus aratro, 40
quem mulcent aurae, firmat sol, educat imber;
multi illum pueri, multae optavere puellae:
idem cum tenui carptus defloruit ungui,
nulli illum pueri, nullae optavere puellae:
sic virgo, dum intacta manet, dum cara suis est; 45
cum castum amisit polluto corpore florem,
nec pueris iucunda manet, nec cara puellis.
Hymen o Hymenaee, Hymen ades o Hymenaee!

49.   This second SIMILE, sung by the young men, follows in the *amoebean* tradition,

       reflecting both the intimacy of comparison that Catullus grasped in the first SIMILE, and also the marriage specific subject matter, which reflects Roman (and indirectly here, Greek) ideology concerning marriage union.

       vidua: viduus, -a, -um, *adj.,* unsupported

       vitis, vitis, *f.,* vine

       arvo: arvus, -i, *adj.,* field

50.   **mitem: mitis, -e,** *adj.,* mild, soft, ripe

       uvam: uva, -ae, *f.,* bunch of grapes

52.   **radice: radix, radicis,** *f.,* root

53.   **coluere: colo,** 3, cultivate, look after (3rd pers. perf.)

       iuvenci: iuvencus, -i, *m.,* bull

54.   **ulmo: ulmus, -i,** *f.,* elm

       marito: maritus, -i, *m.,* husband

56.   **inculta: incultus, -a, -um,** *adj.,* unkempt

       senescit: senesco, 3, grow old

57.   **adepta est: adipiscor, adipisci, adeptus,** obtain (*lit.* to come up to)

58.   **invisa: invisus, -a, -um,** hated

60.   **aequom = aequum:** fair

63.   **patrist = patri est** (*a* is long)

65.   **iura: ius, iuris,** *n.,* right

       dote: dos, dotis, *f.,* dowry

Ut vidua in nudo vitis quae nascitur arvo,
numquam se extollit, numquam mitem educat uvam,　　　50
sed tenerum prono deflectens pondere corpus
iam iam contingit summum radice flagellum;
hanc nulli agricolae, nulli coluere iuvenci:
at si forte eadem est ulmo coniuncta marito,
multi illam agricolae, multi coluere iuvenci:　　　55
sic virgo dum intacta manet, dum inculta senescit;
cum par conubium maturo tempore adepta est,
cara viro magis et minus est invisa parenti.
<Hymen o Hymenaee, Hymen ades o Hymenaee!>

Et tu ne pugna cum tali coniuge, virgo.
non aequom est pugnare, pater cui tradidit ipse,　　　60
ipse pater cum matre, quibus parere necesse est.
virginitas non tota tua est, ex parte parentum est;
tertia pars patrist, pars est data tertia matri,
tertia sola tua est: noli pugnare duobus,
qui genero sua iura simul cum dote dederunt.　　　65
Hymen o Hymenaee, Hymen ades o Hymenaee!

Catullus 70: Notes

Meter: Elegiac Couplet

This poem ends with a rather common poetic lament regarding a woman changing her mind. The image of writing on wind and/or water is an ancient METAPHOR for mutability, dating back to Plato, at least. Compare its use by Catullus here with a rather different watery concept by Horace, in his *Ode* 1.5.

1. **nubere: nubo,** 3, marry; here, as a complimentary infinitive for **malle,** which is itself an indirect statement infinitive with **dicit.**

   Note the ALLITERATION with **mulier mea... malle mihi,** which gives a sound of contentment with what his woman "says" she wants. Compare this with the ANAPHORA in **dicit.** Clearly, at issue is whether the poet can believe what his woman says.

2. **non si,** idiom: not even if. Use of this expression in this context has special overtones, since Jupiter was known for his seduction of humans and immortals alike; but Catullus's girl (she says) would refuse even him.

   petat: here, as a potential subjunctive governed by **non si,** since Jupiter has not asked, but if he did....

4. **oportet,** *impers.*: **oportet,** 2, it is proper, one should, one ought to. The suggestion is firm, but not overbearing; it is fluid and evasive, like the water and wind METAPHOR it employs.

CATULLUS 70

Nulli se dicit mulier mea nubere malle
  quam mihi, non si se Iuppiter ipse petat.
dicit: sed mulier cupido quod dicit amanti,
  in vento et rapida scribere oportet aqua.

Catullus 72: Notes

Meter: Elegiac Couplet

In this poem we have the sad sequel to Poem 70. Catullus begins this poem with "You once said..." and he proceeds to lament that he should have known better, should not have loved so completely; now that he knows her, his love for her has changed.

1.   **quondam,** *adv.,* once, formerly, at a certain time. The use of this adverb with **dicebas** sets the poignant tone for this piece.

     nosse: nosco, 3, know, become acquainted with. The form **nosse** is the syncopated perfect infinitive **novisse.**

2.   **prae,** *prep. + abl.,* before

     velle, *inf.:* indirect statement following **dicebas** in 1, as was **nosse.**

     tenere, *inf.: teneo* means "to hold" but it also carries the meaning of "to hold onto," "to possess," or "to belong to"

     Note that the word order in the first couplet is very straightforward; it is as though the poet is speaking quietly, directly, sadly, without flourish.

3.   **dilexi: diligo,** 3, love, esteem highly. We can liken this to our METAPHOR of placing someone on a pedestal. The idea gains weight when compounded with the next line where Catullus' relationship with Lesbia is likened to that of a father and son. This relationship in Rome was more than biological: it was sacred.

     vulgus, -i, *n.,* crowd or common people; *as a substantive:* common man

4.   **gnatos = natos, natus, -i,** *m.,* son, child; can be taken as "daughters" as well. It would

seem that Catullus chose **gnatos** instead of the more common *natos* so that it made the point he fortified with the following word: **generos.**

generos: gener, generi, *m.,* a son-in-law

Since the husband of his daughter would also be held in high esteem by a father, familial affection is clearly Catullus' desired relationship reference. It is intended to express both the depth and extent of emotion Catullus felt for Lesbia.

5.   **cognovi: cognosco,** 3, know, as *nosco* above. The fact that Catullus uses a different word, however, implies a different kind of knowledge; for example, "now I know you again, or in a different light:" "Now I know the 'real' you."

     quare, *adv.,* therefore, so

     etsi, *conj.,* although, notwithstanding

     impensius: impense, *adv.,* intensely, urgently

6.   **vilior: vilis, -e,** *adj.,* cheap

7.   **qui potis est: Qui,** here, as an adverb, means "how." The phrase is idiomatic: "How is that possible?"

Catullus 72

Dicebas quondam solum te nosse Catullum,
    Lesbia, nec prae me velle tenere Iovem.
dilexi tum te non tantum ut vulgus amicam,
    sed pater ut gnatos diligit et generos.
nunc te cognovi: quare etsi impensius uror,   5
    multo mi tamen es vilior et levior.
qui potis est, inquis? quod amantem iniuria talis
    cogit amare magis, sed bene velle minus.

CATULLUS 83, 85: NOTES

Meter: Elegiac Couplet

This poem presents the reader with a curious bit of "lover logic." Since Lesbia cannot refrain from speaking ill of Catullus at every opportunity, especially in front of her husband, this is an indication that the poet is always on her mind. She could not logically praise him to her husband since the man would suspect; therefore, she loves him!

1. **praesente: praesum esse,** *pres. part.,* being present; ablative absolute

   viro: There is generally a note on this poem indicating that, assuming Lesbia is the famous Clodia, then the **viro** here is Quintus Metellus Celer, who was consul in 60 BC.

2. **haec:** "This thing is **(est)**" (nom. sing. fem.)

   fatuo: fatuus, -a, -um, silly, stupid; here, used as a substantive

3. **mule: mulus, -i,** *m.,* mule (APOSTROPHE to **viro**)

   The term is clearly intended as derogatory by its accompaniment with **nihil sentis.** The effect is enhanced by the undoubtedly prominent position that Lesbia's husband must have had in Roman society.

   oblita: obliviscor, *dep.,* forget

4. **sana: sanus, -a, -um,** *adj.,* healthy, sane, sober

   gannit: gannio, 4, snarl or growl

   obloquitur: obloquor, *dep.,* speak against

5. **meminit: memini, -isse,** *defective: perfect with a sense of present,* remember, recollect

   quae multo acrior est res: idiomatic, literally, "the thing much sharper (more to the point) is..."

6. **uritur: uro, 3,** burn; be on fire (with anger or passion)

   et: here, "and so"

Meter: Elegiac Couplet

This poem is a masterpiece of lyric poetry: fourteen words, eight of them verbs; no nouns or adjectives: pure, intensely personal emotion.

1. **quare:** how, why
2. **fieri: fio, fieri, factus,** *here,* happen, become

excrucior: excrucio, 1, be in agony, torment

Catullus 83

Lesbia mi praesente viro mala plurima dicit:
  haec illi fatuo maxima laetitia est.
mule, nihil sentis? si nostri oblita taceret,
  sana esset: nunc quod gannit et obloquitur,
non solum meminit, sed, quae multo acrior est res, 5
  irata est. hoc est, uritur et loquitur.

Catullus 85

Odi et amo. quare id faciam, fortasse requiris?
  nescio, sed fieri sentio et excrucior.

Catullus 86, 87: Notes

Meter: Elegiac Couplet

In this piece, Catullus counters those who extol the charms of a woman named Quintia who is unknown in Roman history, but serves here as a comparative persona placed opposite the flowering persona of Lesbia. Note especially the pairs of words from lines 3–6 which enhance the comparisons being made between the two women: **nam nulla...nulla...; Formosa est...pulcherrima tota est; omnibus...omnis.**

1. **candida:** In the strictest sense this adj. means "white," but in reference to a woman and, especially in Catullus' poetry, the word refers to a woman's complexion and skin tone. In Rome, of course, the custom was "the lighter the better," which is why women used white lead in their makeup.

2. **recta: rectus, -a, -um,** *adj., from* **rego,** 3, straight, well-ruled; here, having good posture

   haec...singula: "these separate or various things," referring to **candida, longa,** and **recta.**

   sic: thus, so

   The term has an air of concession: **candida, longa** and **recta** are some of the determining factors in assessing **formosa,** which Catullus admits; however there are additional influences in determining true beauty which Catullus addresses.

   confiteor, *dep.,* confess, admit

3. **illud:** refers to **candida, longa,** etc., the physical characteristics. "I deny all that constitutes beauty."

   venustas, venustatis *from* **Venus, Veneris,** *f.,* charm, loveliness, grace

3–4. **est:** is taken individually with **nulla venustas,** and separately with **nulla mica salis.**

4. **mica, -ae,** *f.,* morsel, grain

   salis: sal, salis, *m.,* salt

5–6. **cum...tum:** an adverbial combination, which forms a correlative (in this case, meaning: "not only...but also") that connects similar ideas in two distinctly different phrases.

6. **Veneres:** these are the qualities that Venus exhibits. Compare to **venustas,** 3, which is of similar linguistic origin and closely related in meaning and function. The distinction between the two is subtle.

Meter: Elegiac Couplet

The poet, unable (or unwilling) to accept that his beloved has broken a bond he considered sacred, sets forth his lament in two couplets. Note the intertwining words throughout the poem, forming a "bond" of their own: *nulla...mulier tantum...amatam...quantum...Lesbia...amata mea....* Yet, in spite of the word order, there is great fluidity, enhancing the effect of sadness.

1. **amatam** (+ *esse*): indirect statement following **dicere**

3. **ullo: ullus, -a, -um,** *adj.,* any (used commonly in hypothetical and negative sentences)

   foedere: foedus, foederis, *n.,* a compact, covenant or agreement

4. **tuo:** dative, "my love for you"

   reperta: reperio, 4, find, obtain again

CATULLUS 86

Quintia formosa est multis. mihi candida, longa,
    recta est: haec ego sic singula confiteor.
totum illud formosa nego: nam nulla venustas,
    nulla in tam magno est corpore mica salis.
Lesbia formosa est, quae cum pulcerrima tota est,   5
    tum omnibus una omnis surripuit Veneres.

CATULLUS 87

Nulla potest mulier tantum se dicere amatam
    vere, quantum a me Lesbia amata mea est.
Nulla fides ullo fuit umquam foedere tanta,
    quanta in amore tuo ex parte reperta mea est.

CATULLUS 92, 109: NOTES

Meter: Elegiac Couplet

Compare this poem with 83, where the poet was trying to convince himself of Lesbia's love in spite of her verbal abuse. Here, continuing in the same vein of logic, he notes that he says horrible things about her as well; he loves her deeply, nonetheless, so.... Note the two significant repetitions in this poem, again employed when Catullus compares two people; in this case, his affection with hers: *Lesbia mi...Lesbia me; dispeream nisi amat...dispeream nisi amo.*

2. **dispeream: dispereo,** 4, perish utterly, be ruined

3. **quo signo:** idiomatic, "what's the proof?" or "What does that signify?"

   quia: because

totidem, *adj. indecl.,* just as many

quia...mea: colloquial, without a specific subject. Translate: "I do the same thing."

4. **assidue,** *adv.,* constantly

Meter: Elegiac Couplet

Many consider this to be the most beautiful elegy in Latin love poetry. The reading is smooth, clear, and pointed. Catullus leaves little doubt about his feelings for Lesbia. Note his word selection, containing elements of that which lasts, which is meaningful, which continues on: **proponis, perpetuum, promittere, sincere, perducere, tota...vita, aeternum.**

1. **iucundum: iucundus, -a, -um,** *adj.,* pleasant, agreeable, delightful

   mea vita: Note the APOSTROPHE. There can be little confusion or doubt about Catullus' feelings for Lesbia.

   proponis: propono, 3, put forth, propose, promise

2. **fore:** fut. act. inf. of *sum*

3. **Di magni:** clearly a prayer, evidenced by **facite ut vere.**

5. **tota...vita:** abl. of duration of time, with **perducere,** which does not require the construction; indeed, an accusative would be usual here.

6. Note that Catullus returns to the "sacred bond" theme that he mentioned in poem 87 and suggested in poem 72. He wants Lesbia, if not the world, to know that he did not consider their affair a transitory flirtation, but something beautiful and sacred.

Catullus 92

Lesbia mi dicit semper male nec tacet umquam
    de me: Lesbia me dispeream nisi amat.
quo signo? quia sunt totidem mea: deprecor illam
    assidue, verum dispeream nisi amo.

Catullus 109

Iucundum, mea vita, mihi proponis amorem
    hunc nostrum inter nos perpetuumque fore.
Di magni, facite ut vere promittere possit,
    atque id sincere dicat et ex animo
ut liceat nobis tota perducere vita   5
    aeternum hoc sanctae foedus amicitiae.

HORACE

Symposium, Campanian bell-krater, fourth century BC.

Photograph by Raymond V. Schroder, S. J.

HORACE

Quintus Horatius Flaccus was born on December 8, 65 BC, in Venusia, a town at the opposite end of Italy from Catullus' Verona. He tells us that he grew up "between Apulia and Lucania," the two areas at the southern end of Italy's boot. The son of a freedman, he nevertheless was educated in Rome and Athens. The young Horace, a student in Athens when Marcus Brutus was seeking support for the restoration of the republic following the assassination of Julius Caesar, joined Brutus' ranks which likely caused his father's estates to be confiscated by Octavian. Since he no longer had lands to farm, he turned to writing as a profession in the form of a clerical job. He became acquainted with Vergil and Varius, and through them, Maecenas. This was a crucial point in Horace's career, for Maecenas was THE patron for poets. Maecenas could provide financial support, but more importantly, he had the ear of Augustus. Horace composed prolifically until his death in 8 BC. His writings include the Odes, Epodes, Satires, Letters, and Ars Poetica.

HORACE *ODES* 1.5: NOTES

Meter: Fourth Asclepiadean

This ode is dedicated to a girl whom the poet knows to be fickle in her affections. Its comparisons to many of the laments of Catullus should be obvious, but see particularly Catullus 70, where the poet complains that the promises made by a woman to her lover should be written on the wind and rapidly-flowing water. Note, however, that while Catullus is sad or embittered regarding his lover's inability to concentrate on one man at a time, Horace seems grateful to have escaped from the relationship relatively unscathed.

1. **quis = qui:** "what"

    multa...in rosa: this CHIASMUS translates best "in/or on a bed of roses"

2. **urget: urgeo,** 2, embrace, press upon

3. **Pyrrha:** a girl's name, derived from the Greek *pyr*, "fire"

    sub: here, "under cover of"

    sub antro: the mention of a cave as meeting place has implications which range from a similarity to the refuge of Dido and Aeneas, to that of a primal trysting place in the womb of Mother Earth.

4. **flavam,** *adj.,* blonde

    religas: religo, 1, tie or bind back

5. **munditiis:** elegance

6. **flebit: fleo,** 2, weep for or mourn

    Note that the subject of **flebit** is **puer,** from 1.

    aspera...ventis: SYNCHYSIS

8. **emirabitur: emiror,** *dep.,* wonder at

    insolens, *adj.,* surprised, inexperienced

9. **fruitur: fruor,** *dep., takes the ablative:* enjoys or delights in

10. **vacuam,** *adj.,* free, available; empty, meaningless

    amabilem, *adj.,* lovely, friendly

12. **fallacis: fallax, fallacis,** *adj.,* deceitful, false

    miseri: supply *sunt*

13. **intemptata:** *adj.,* untried

    nites: niteo, 2, shine, sparkle

13–16. **me tabula...deo:** In gratitude for surviving a shipwreck, sailors might hang their drenched clothing on a temple wall with a tablet, or sign, thanking the god of the sea for allowing them to escape with their lives. The student should note that **sacer** and **paries** are *nom.,* **tabula** and **votiva,** *abl.* If this were in English word order, it might read: **Sacer paries (votiva tabula) indicat me uvida vestimenta suspendisse potenti deo maris.**

Horace *Odes* 1.5

Quis multa gracilis te puer in rosa
perfusus liquidis urget odoribus
    grato, Pyrrha, sub antro ?
        cui flavam religas comam,

simplex munditiis? heu quotiens fidem   5
mutatosque deos flebit et aspera
    nigris aequora ventis
        emirabitur insolens,

qui nunc te fruitur credulus aurea,
qui semper vacuam, semper amabilem   10
    sperat, nescius aurae
        fallacis! miseri, quibus

intemptata nites. me tabula sacer
votiva paries indicat uvida
    suspendisse potenti   15
        vestimenta maris deo.

HORACE *ODES* 1.11: NOTES

Meter: Fifth Asclepiadean

This poem expresses a theme popular among many poets: "Seize the Day!" Note particularly Catullus 5: "Let us live, my Lesbia, and let us love...." and Ben Johnson's poem to Celia: "Come, my Celia, let us prove while we may, the sports of love; time will not be ours forever...." Robert Herrick also advised: "...Then be not coy, but use your time, and, while ye may, go marry..." and Andrew Marvell urged his coy mistress to "...let us sport us while we may...." This last poem by Marvell also emphasizes the pressures of time: "Had we but world enough, and time, this coyness lady were no crime..." which echoes Horace's **invida aetas,** which has fled even while we speak, in line 7.

1. **ne quaesieris...nec...temptaris: ne** with these perfect subjunctives can be used as an alternative (and perhaps, more personal) negative imperative to **noli** + inf.

   nefas, *n. indecl.,* crime, sin; here, supply *est* for clarity

2. **finem:** goes with both **quem mihi** and **quem tibi**

   di: syncopated form of **dei,** nom. pl.

   Leuconoe, Leuconoes, *f.,* a woman's name, from the Greek *leukos,* meaning white or bright; and from *nous,* meaning mind. Obviously a girl with such a "bright mind" can see the logic in the poet's argument.

   Babylonios...numeros: a reference to Chaldaean astrological calculations; hence, she was checking her horoscope.

3. **temptaris = temptaveris**

4. **hiemes:** here, METONYMY; "many winters" for "many years"

   tribuit: tribuo, 3, allocate, grant

5. **debilitat: debilito,** 1, weaken or break down

   pumicibus: pumex, pumicis, *m.,* pumice stone

6. **sapias...liques...reseces:** three interesting pieces of advice in the form of iussive subjunctives, considering that the ablative **spatio brevi** is inserted before the **spem longam** she is urged to cut back upon.

   sapias: sapio, 3, be wise, show good sense

   liques: liquo, 1, strain the wine, decant the wine

   spatio brevi: ablative of cause

7. **reseces: reseco,** 1, cut back, restrain, cut short

   invida: *adj.,* envious, grudging

8. **quam minimum:** as little as possible

   credulus, -a, -um, *adj.* (+ dative), trusting in, believing easily

Horace *Odes* 1.11

Tu ne quaesieris, scire nefas, quem mihi, quem tibi
finem di dederint, Leuconoe, nec Babylonios
temptaris numeros. ut melius, quidquid erit, pati,
seu pluris hiemes seu tribuit Iuppiter ultimam,
quae nunc oppositis debilitat pumicibus mare   5
Tyrrhenum: sapias, vina liques, et spatio brevi
spem longam reseces. dum loquimur, fugerit invida
aetas: carpe diem, quam minimum credula postero.

HORACE *ODES* 1.22: NOTES

Meter: Sapphic

This poem, pointing out that a man of purity may go through life armed only with his love, is in Sapphic meter, like Catullus 11 and 51. Like Catullus 11, Horace includes a catalogue of place names from what were (in Roman times) the farthest ends of the earth; also, he addresses his comments to his close friends Furius and Aurelius (Horace addresses this poem to Fuscus). Unlike Catullus, however, Horace is secure in the love of his girl. Catullus 51 is a close parallel to fragment 31 of a poem by Sappho. Worth noting is the mention here of the "sweetly laughing, sweetly talking" Lalage (a name which, in Greek, means to "babble" or "chatter"). These are attributes of the objects of Catullus' and Sappho's poems.

1. **integer:** *adj.*, here with the genitive of reference or respect, with **vitae.** Meaning "innocent," "whole," "complete," or "pure," its placement as the first word in the poem is significant, and the noun which it is intended to modify, man, is understood.

    scelus, -eris, *n.*, wickedness. Here a genitive with the adj. **purus**

    Note the CHIASMUS in this line.

2. **Mauris:** Moorish, African

    iaculis: iaculum, -i, *n.*, dart, javelin

    egit: egeo, egere, egui, 2, need (+ abl.)

3. SYNCHYSIS with poisoned arrows and full quiver

    venenatis, *adj.*, poisoned

4. **Fusce,** *vocative* (a reference to Aristius Fuscus, who was a close friend of Horace)

    pharetra: quiver (a container full of arrows carried by a hunter)

5. **Syrtes:** the proper name of the sand banks on the North African coast between Carthage and Cyrene.

    aestuosus, -a, -um, *adj.*, hot, steamy, heat-filled

6. **facturus:** *fut. part. of* **facio.** Supply *est* and read with **iter.**

7. **Caucasum:** a reference to the mountain range east of the Black Sea

    fabulosus, -a, -um, *adj.*, legendary

8. **lambit: lambo,** 3, lick, lap or splash

    Hydaspes, Hydaspis, *m.*, a tributary of the Indus River

9. **Sabina,** *adj.*, reference to the Sabine Hills, an area in central Italy where Horace had a farm.

10. **Lalagen** (*Greek acc.*): **Lalage, -es,** *f.*, a woman's name, meaning "chatter" or "prattle," appropriate for the **loquentem Lalagen.**

    ultra, *prep. + acc.*, beyond, farther than

11. **vagor, vagari, vagatus sum,** *dep.*, wander, roam freely

12. **inermem,** *adj.*, unarmed

13. **portentum,- i,** *n.*, portent, omen, something unnatural

14. **Daunias, Dauniadis,** *f.: derived from* **Daunus, -i,** *m.*: a legendary king of Apulia. Venusia, whence Horace came, is near Apulia, in southern Italy.

    latus, -a, -um, *adj.*, wide, broad

    alit: alo, alere, alui, alitum, 3, nourish, nurse, cherish

    aesculetis: aesculetum, -i, *n.*, an oak forest

15. **Iubae: Iuba, -ae,** *m.*, the king of Numidia in Horace's time. Numidia, of course, was famous for its lions.

16. **nutrix:** nurse

    arida nuxtrix: an OXYMORON in itself, a TRANSFERRED EPITHET with **tellus**

17. **pigris:** read [*in*] **pigris ...campis**

18. **aestiva,** *adj.*, summer

    recreatur: recreo, 1, restore, revive

19. Read: **latus mundi quod...**

19–20. **malusque Iuppiter** implies "gloomy skies" by METONOMY

20. **urget: urgeo,** 2, press upon or embrace

21. **nimium propinqui:** "much too near." The poet is asking to be placed where the sun chariot passes closest to the earth, an area "denied habitation"

22. **domibus: domus, -us** or **-i,** *dative with* **negata**

    negata: nego, 1, deny, refuse, decline

HORACE ODES 1.22

Integer vitae scelerisque purus
non eget Mauris iaculis neque arcu
nec venenatis gravida sagittis,
    Fusce, pharetra,

sive per Syrtis iter aestuosas   5
sive facturus per inhospitalem
Caucasum vel quae loca fabulosus
    lambit Hydaspes.

namque me silva lupus in Sabina,
dum meam canto Lalagen et ultra   10
terminum curis vagor expeditis,
    fugit inermem,

quale portentum neque militaris
Daunias latis alit aesculetis
nec Iubae tellus generat, leonum   15
    arida nutrix.

pone me pigris ubi nulla campis
arbor aestiva recreatur aura,
quod latus mundi nebulae malusque
    Iuppiter urget;   20

pone sub curru nimium propinqui
solis in terra domibus negata:
dulce ridentem Lalagen amabo,
    dulce loquentem.

HORACE *ODES* 1.23: NOTES

Meter: Fourth Asclepiadean

Chloe, the object of this poem, takes her name from the Greek word for a green twig, or a newly-sprouted leaf. The combination of the woods and animal references in this poem presents the suggestion that one might think of Daphne, or other follower of Diana, running from a persistent suitor. Compare Horace's METAPHOR here of Chloe as a fawn, with Ovid's telling of Daphne's interaction with Apollo in *Metamorphoses* 1.504–524, as the god tries to convince his fleeing love that he is not an enemy pursuing her; she has nothing to fear.

1. **inuleo** (*also* **hinnuleo**): *dat. with* **similis,** a fawn

    Chloe: Greek vocative. Note that the *oe* here is *not* a diphthong.

2. **pavidam:** *adj.,* frightened, trembling

    aviis: *adj.,* pathless, having no road or pathway

3. **vano:** *adj.,* empty, useless

    non sine: LITOTES

4. **silvae:** use **siluae** and scan as three syllables

5. **veris: ver, veris,** *n.,* spring

    inhorruit: inhorresco, 3, begin to tremble (inceptive verb)

6. **adventus:** here, in the nominative

    rubum: rubus, -i, *m.,* bramble or thorn bush

7. **dimovere = dimoverunt**

    lacertae: lacerta, -ae, *f.,* lizard

8. **genibus: genu, -us,** *n.,* knee

9. **atqui,** *conj.,* nevertheless, and yet, but

10. **Gaetulus,- a, -um,** *adj.,* pertaining to Gaetulia (a region in N.W. Africa)

    persequor: read as **persequor (ut) frangere** (inf. of purpose)

11. **desine** (*imp.*): **desino,** 3, stop, cease

12. **tempestiva:** supply *es*

HORACE *ODES* 1.23

Vitas inuleo me similis, Chloe,
quaerenti pavidam montibus aviis
    matrem non sine vano
        aurarum et silvae metu.

nam seu mobilibus veris inhorruit   5
adventus foliis seu virides rubum
    dimovere lacertae,
        et corde et genibus tremit.

atqui non ego te tigris ut aspera
Gaetulusve leo frangere persequor;   10
    tandem desine matrem
        tempestiva sequi viro.

HORACE *ODES* 1.25: NOTES

Meter: Sapphic

In this poem, Lydia has moved on to a new relationship—or at any rate she has refused the poet. He warns her that not for long will she find herself pursued by young men and she will be a withered old woman weeping in alley-ways. There are echoes of Catullus here, particularly in Catullus 8, where that poet berates himself in the first half of the poem and then turns his anger to Lesbia from line 12 on, with a series of rhetorical questions wondering who will be attracted to her when he is gone.

1. **parcius** (*comp. adverb*): more sparingly, less often, less frequently

   iunctas (*part.*) **iungo, 3,** joined; here, closed, shuttered

2. **iactibus: iactus, -us,** *m.,* things which are thrown, cast

   protervi, *adj.,* bold, impudent

3. **tibi** (*dat. with* **adimo**): here, "from you"

5. **multum,** *adv.,* much

6. **cardines:** hinges

7. **pereunte** (*pres. part. of* **pereo**): here, "being desperately in love with"

9. **invicem,** *adv.,* by turns, alternately

   moechos: moechus, -i, *m.,* adulterer

   anus, -us, *f.,* old woman

10. **in solo...angiportu:** in a lonely (or deserted) alley

    levis: "fickle," "capricious," or "trivial"; note that it goes with **anus**

11. **Thracio: Thracius, -a, -um,** *adj.,* of Thrace (a region north of Greece particularly associated with the cult of Bacchus, and considered a bit wild)

    bacchante (*pres. part.*) *from* **bacchor, -ari, -atus,** *dep.,* rave, riot, run wild (like a follower of Bacchus)

    interlunia: interlunium, -i, *n., literally,* between the moon (phases); the time of the dark of the moon, before the crescent begins to wax anew

13. **tibi:** dat. of reference

    libido, libidinis, *f.,* lust

14. **matres...equorum:** mothers of horses. Horace is behaving a bit uncharitably, equating Lydia with a mare in heat

15. **iecur, iecoris,** *n.,* liver (once thought to be the center of passion)

16. **non sine:** LITOTES

    questu: questus, -us, *m.,* complaint, moan

17. **pubes, -is,** *f.,* here, the adult male population as a whole

    virenti (*pres. part.*): **vireo, 2,** becoming green

18. **pulla,** *adj.,* dark, sad

    atque: may be translated "than" with comparatives

    myrto: myrtus, -i, *f.,* myrtle (an evergreen plant held sacred to Venus: the flowers were often woven into bridal wreaths, the berries chewed to sweeten the breath)

19. **hiemis: hiems, hiemis,** *f.,* winter, winter storms

    sodali: sodalis, -is, *m.,* companion

20. **Euro: Eurus, -i,** *m.,* the East wind

Horace *Odes* 1.25

Parcius iunctas quatiunt fenestras
iactibus crebris iuvenes protervi,
nec tibi somnos adimunt, amatque
    ianua limen,

quae prius multum facilis movebat   5
cardines; audis minus et minus iam
"me tuo longas pereunte noctes,
    Lydia, dormis?"

invicem moechos anus arrogantes
flebis in solo levis angiportu,   10
Thracio bacchante magis sub inter-
    lunia vento,

cum tibi flagrans amor et libido,
quae solet matres furiare equorum,
saeviet circa iecur ulcerosum   15
    non sine questu

laeta quod pubes hedera virenti
gaudeat pulla magis atque myrto,
aridas frondes hiemis sodali
    dedicet Euro.*   20

*In some MSS. this is *Hebro,* a river in Thrace

HORACE *ODES* 2.4: NOTES

Meter: Sapphic & Adonic

In this poem Horace speaks to a friend, here in direct address, *Xanthia Phoceu,* but perhaps since the adjective *xanthias* in Greek means "blonde," he is referring to a man with the Roman name *Flavius* (also meaning blonde). At any rate, he is urging his friend not be ashamed of his affection for his serving girl, since many great men before him had acknowledged the same ties. He also points out that this girl may, in fact, have come from a great family in whatever country she had been enslaved. This provides an interesting look at the slavery issue in the ever-expanding Roman Empire.

1. **pudori: pudor,** shame. Here, dative of purpose

2. **Xanthia Phoceu** (*Greek vocative*)

    insolentem: insolens, *adj.,* arrogant, excessive sense of self

3. **Briseis:** Achilles' captive slave girl in the *Iliad* over whom the warrior brooded inconsolably when Agamemnon took her for himself

    niveo: snow-white

    colore: here, read as "complexion" rather than as "color"

5. **Aiacem Telemone** (**Telemone** = *abl. of origin*): Ajax, son of Telamon, a Greek warrior known for his bravery and skill in the Trojan War

    natum: natus, -i, *m.,* son

6. **Tecmessae:** daughter of the king of Thrace. Ajax took her when he killed her father in a battle.

    captivae dominum: ANTITHESIS

7. **arsit: ardeo,** 2, burn, be inflamed (here, with passion)

    Atrides: a patronymic, here referring to Agamemnon, son of Atreus

8. **virgine rapta** (*abl. of cause with* **ardeo**): The "maiden seized" in this reference is, of course, Cassandra, daughter of Priam, the maiden captured at the fall of Troy and taken by Agamemnon back to Mycenae.

9. **cecidere:** 3rd pl. perf. of **cado**

    turmae: turma, -ae, *f.,* squadron, cavalry, troops in general

10. **Thessalo victore** (*abl. of instrument with* **cecidere**): Thessaly's victor is Achilles. His father Peleus was King of Thessaly.

    ademptus: adimo, 3, take away, remove, deprive

11. **leviora** (*comp. of* **levis**), lighter, easier

    tolli: passive inf.

12. **Pergama:** of Troy, literally, the citadel of Troy; Trojan by METONYMY

    Grais: Graius, -a, -um, *adj.,* Greek

13. **generum: gener, -i,** *m.,* son-in-law

14. **decorent: decoro,** 1, adorn, glorify, honor

    Phyllidis: Greek, gen. sing. with **flavae**

15. **regium:** supply *est*

16. **maeret: maereo,** 2, grieve, bewail

    iniquos: *adj.,* unkind, hostile. Her Penates are deemed **iniquos** because instead of protecting the household, they allowed the girl to be sold into slavery.

18. **plebe: plebes, -ei,** *f.,* common person, plebeian

    dilectam: diligo, 3, esteem, hold dear

19. **lucro** (*abl.*): **lucrum, -i,** *n.,* greed

    aversam: *adj.,* turned from, disinclined toward

20. **pudenda:** shameful (here, referring to her birth)

21. **vultum: vultus, -us,** *m.,* face or expression (also written *voltus*)

    teretes: elegant

    suras: calves (of the legs)

23. **octavum...lustrum:** fortieth year

    lustrum,- i, *n.,* a five-year period of time

Horace *Odes* 2.4

Ne sit ancillae tibi amor pudori,
Xanthia Phoceu, prius insolentem
serva Briseis niveo colore
    movit Achillem;

movit Aiacem Telamone natum   5
forma captivae dominum Tecmessae;
arsit Atrides medio in triumpho
    virgine rapta,

barbarae postquam cecidere turmae
Thessalo victore et ademptus Hector   10
tradidit fessis leviora tolli
    Pergama Grais.

nescias an te generum beati
Phyllidis flavae decorent parentes:
regium certe genus et penatis   15
    maeret iniquos.

crede non illam tibi de scelesta
plebe delectam, neque sic fidelem,
sic lucro aversam potuisse nasci
    matre pudenda.   20

bracchia et vultum teretesque suras
integer laudo; fuge suspicari
cuius octavum trepidavit aetas
    claudere lustrum.

HORACE *ODES* 2.12: Notes

Meter: Third Asclepiadean

When Augustus celebrated his triumphs in Actium, Pannonia, and Egypt, his friend Maecenas called upon his client Horace to write a commemorative piece in praise of Augustus' military prowess. It would seem that Horace begged to be excused from the task, saying that his kind of verse was not suited to history, but rather to love. He chose instead to praise a lady whom he named Licymnia, whom many scholars feel was a pseudonym for Maecenas' wife, Terentia. Compare this poem with the first of Ovid's *Amores*, wherein that poet complains that he intended to write grand epic verse, but that due to a spiteful Cupid, he had a foot of the dactylic hexameter stolen and he was forced instead to write in elegiac couplets, turning out love poetry instead. This type of poem has been called a **recusatio,** in that the poet is refusing, or rejecting, a challenge; usually this involves the subject claiming disqualification due to interest or bias.

1. **Numantiae:** Numantia, a town in Spain. The interlocked word order in this line complements the reference to the convoluted eight-year siege by P. Scipio Aemilienus in 143 BC.

    nolis: a potential subjunctive, used more as a suggestion, and could be translated: "you (or, as an indef., "one") would not wish..."

2. **durum:** harsh, vigorous, burdensome (all meanings appropriate to the Roman views of Hannibal, who harassed Rome continually for almost twenty years)

    Siculum: *adj.,* Sicilian

3. **Poeno:** *adj.,* Punic, Carthaginian. The reference to the Sicilian sea, purple with Punic blood, is full of IRONY; the dye which made the finest purple color in antiquity came originally from Phoenicia, origin of Carthage, hence the word Punic.

4. **aptari** (*pass. inf.*): **apto,** 1, fit, apply; here, a complement to **nolis** in 1

    citharae: the lyre, an instrument for accompanying lyric poetry

5. **Lapithas:** This reference is to a drunken brawl between the Lapithae (a legendary tribe in Thessaly) and the Centaurs at the wedding feast of Pirithous and Hippodamia.

    nimium: excessive, immoderate, too much

6. **Hylaeum:** Hylaeus was a centaur from the same battle

    domitos: domo, -are, -ui, -itus, 1, tame or subdue

    Herculea: *adj.,* Herculean, pertaining to Hercules

7. **Telluris: tellus, telluris,** *f.,* the earth. The **iuvenes telluris** (or sons of the earth) were the giants, whom Tellus (Mother Earth) had defended against divine interference, but who were vulnerable by mortal hands—hence, by Hercules.

8. **contremuit: contremo, -ere,** 3, tremble or quake

9. **Saturni:** Saturnus, father of Jupiter and the other Olympians; the implication is that Hercules posed a threat to the shining house of all the gods.

    pedestribus...historiis: "historical feet"; this is a reference to poetic meter; Horace feels that it would be best to describe all of these historical events that he has just catalogued (in reverse chronological order, by the way) in dactylic hexameter or prose, rather than in lyric measures.

11. **Maecenas** (*voc.*): Horace tells his mentor that he would do a much better **(melius)** job writing Caesar's battles than Horace can.

12. **minacium: minax, minacis,** *adj.,* threatening

    colla: collum, -i, *n.,* neck. This is a reference to the victory parades following a war, during which enemy kings were led through the streets with chains around their necks. This is the kind of parade, of course, which Augustus was about to have, occasioning the request for this poem.

HORACE ODES 2.12

Nolis longa ferae bella Numantiae
nec durum Hannibalem nec Siculum mare
Poeno purpureum sanguine mollibus
    aptari citharae modis,

nec saevos Lapithas et nimium mero   5
Hylaeum domitosque Herculea manu
Telluris iuvenes, unde periculum
    fulgens contremuit domus

Saturni veteris; tuque pedestribus
dices historiis proelia Caesaris,   10
Maecenas, melius ductaque per vias
    regum colla minacium.

13. **me:** This pronoun, placed in contrast to **tu** in 9, clearly separates the tasks Horace perceives for himself and Maecenas: You are best suited to writing in historical meters, but me the Muses wish to express the sweet singing, etc.

     Licymniae: dominae Licymniae is no doubt Terentia, Maecenas' new wife.

     dulces...cantus: note CHIASMUS with **dominae Licymniae**

14. **cantus, -us,** *m.,* song

     lucidum, *adj.,* bright, clear, here, "brightly" with **fulgentes** (poetic acc. as adv.)

15. **mutuis...amoribus:** CHIASMUS with **fidum pectus**

16. **pectus, pectoris,** *n.,* breast, soul, understanding

17. **dedecuit: dedecet, dedecuit,** *impers.,* it is unsuitable for or unbecoming to; taken with **nec** it becomes a LITOTES

     choris: chorus, -i, *m.,* a dance with singing, chorus, band

18. **certare:** compete against; have a competition; here, in humor (**ioco**)

19. **ludentem: ludo,** 3, play, sport, banter

20. **celebris: celeber, -bris, -bre,** filled, crowded; TRANSFERRED EPITHET from the temple to the goddess herself

21. **Achaemenes:** legendary founder of a Persian royal line, famous for his incredible wealth

22. **Mygdonias:** *adj.,* regarding Mygdon, an early Phrygian king; hence, **pinguis Phyrgiae** = fertile (not "fat") Phrygia.

23. **velis** (*subjunctive of* **volo**)

24. **Arabum:** Arabian

25. **detorquet:** "turns aside," here it is perhaps best rendered as "bends," for she bends her neck to...

26. **saevitia:** cruelty; note the OXYMORON in combining this with **facili**

27. **poscente** (*pres. part.*): **posco,** 3, request, demand, require

28. **occupet (occupat,** *in some texts*): seize, anticipate, be first to do something

     interdum: now and then

nitidis, -e, *adj.,* shining, flourishing; here, in their festal garments

me dulces dominae Musa Licymniae
cantus, me voluit dicere lucidum
fulgentis oculos et bene mutuis   15
      fidum pectus amoribus,

quam nec ferre pedem dedecuit choris
nec certare ioco nec dare bracchia
ludentem nitidis virginibus sacro
      Dianae celebris die.   20

num tu quae tenuit dives Achaemenes
aut pinguis Phrygiae Mygdonias opes
permutare velis crine Licymniae,
      plenas aut Arabum domos,

cum flagrantia detorquet ad oscula   25
cervicem aut facili saevitia negat,
quae poscente magis gaudeat eripi,
      interdum rapere occupet?

HORACE *ODES* 3.9: NOTES

Meter: Second Asclepiadean

This is a conversational poem; while Horace did not designate the speakers in his text, that has been added here, for purposes of clarity. The style, while not identical to the tone in Catullus 45, compares in its casual, conversational approach.

1. *The poet begins.*

   Donec, *adv.,* as long as

2. **potior:** (*comp. adj. from* **potis**), better, preferable

   candidae: candidus, -a, -um, *adj.,* white, glittering white

3. **cervici: cervix, cervicis,** *f.,* the neck (particularly the nape)

4. **vigui: vigeo,** 2, thrive or flourish

   Persarum: reference to the "King of Persians" is here a METAPHOR for excessive wealth and luxury

5. *Lydia responds to this.*

7. **multi...nominis** (*gen. of quality*)

8. **Ilia** (*abl. of comparison*): another name for Rhea Silvia, mother of Romulus and Remus and (perhaps more to the point in this reference) paramour of Mars, according to Livy.

9. *He speaks again.*

   regit: rego, 3, rule or govern

   Thraessa: Thressa, -ae, *f.:* here, an adj., "Thracian"

10. **docta:** *p. part. of* **doceo,** 2, taught or skilled

    modos: referring to measures or rhythm of poetry

    citharae (*gen. with adj. dep. upon* **sciens**)

    sciens (*pres. part.*): **scio, -ire,** 4, knowing, being versed in, understanding

11. **metuam: metuo, -ere,** 3, fear, be afraid

    mori: morior, die

12. **parcent animae: parco, -ere,** 3, (+ *dative*), spare; in this case **animae,** METONYMY for "she who is the breath of life—or love of my life—to me"

superstiti (*dat.*): **superstes, superstitis,** *adj.,* standing over, surviving; using this form suggests a PROLEPSIS, anticipating that she would be taken from the poet by the Fates

13. *She answers.*

    torret: torreo, -ere, 2, burn, dry up

    face: fax, facis, *f.,* torch (here, "of love")

14. CHIASMUS

15. **patiar:** *subjunctive of* **patior:** suffer or undergo (here, with the infinitive, it has the force of one's being willing to die)

16. Note the parallel construction with 12.

17. *He asks her, "what if...?"*

    prisca: priscus, -a, -um, *adj.,* old-fashioned, former, previous; the "former Venus" is here METONYMY for "our old—former—love"

18. **aeneo,** *adj.,* made of copper or bronze

    diductos (*p. part.*): **diduco, -ere,** 3, draw apart or separate; *hence,* "those who were separated"

19. **excutitur: excutio,** 3, shake out, throw out, shake off

21. *She answers him; obviously what he wants to hear.*

    sidere: *n.,* **sidus, sideris,** *abl. of comparison*

22. **cortice: cortex, corticis,** *m. and f.,* bark, shell; here, cork

    iracundior (*comp. adj.*): **iracundus, -a, -um,** *adj.,* inclined to anger or rage

23. **Hadria: Hadria, -ae,** *m.,* Adriatic Sea

24. **obeam: obeo,** 4, go against or to; here, die

HORACE ODES 3.9

Donec gratus eram tibi
nec quisquam potior bracchia candidae
    cervici iuvenis dabat,
Persarum vigui rege beatior.

"donec non alia magis   5
arsisti neque erat Lydia post Chloen,
    multi Lydia nominis
Romana vigui clarior Ilia."

me nunc Thraessa Chloe regit,
dulcis docta modos et citharae sciens,   10
    pro qua non metuam mori,
si parcent animae fata superstiti.

"me torret face mutua
Thurini Calais filius Ornyti,
    pro quo bis patiar mori,   15
si parcent puero fata superstiti."

quid si prisca redit Venus
diductosque iugo cogit aeneo,
    si flava excutitur Chloe
reiectaeque patet ianua Lydiae?   20

"quamquam sidere pulchrior
ille est, tu levior cortice et improbo
    iracundior Hadria,
tecum vivere amem, tecum obeam libens."

HORACE *ODES* 3.10: NOTES

Meter: Third Asclepiadean

In this poem, Horace complains of an extrordinarily cruel girl named Lyce ("wolf," in Greek) who shuts out her lover in the cold night. This is a common complaint in a poem of this type (called a *paraklausithyron*), with the excluded lover languishing on the doorstep (see *Odes* I.25). Ovid makes reference to a lover camped at his lady's door in *Amores* 1.9. Horace points out that this particular girl is Etruscan; therefore she should be more liberal, rather than conservative like the faithful, waiting wife of Odysseus, Penelope.

1. **Tanain** (*Greek acc.*): a river in ancient Scythia (now in the area of the Ukraine; the river is named the Don)

    si biberes, Lyce: contrary to fact, since Lyce would not be drinking from the Tanais, a reference which here is like saying "the ends of the earth"

2. **saevo...viro:** if she lived in faraway Scythia, she might be married to a savage man

    saevus, -a, -um, *adj.*, savage, raging, ferocious

    asperas: *adj.*, harsh, cruel

3. **porrectum: porrigo, -ere,** 3, stretched or spread out

    The poet has (figuratively speaking) thrown himself at her doorstep.

    obicere: obicio, -ere, 3, throw before

4. **plorares: ploro, -are,** 1, weep aloud, wail

    Aquilonibus: Aquilo, -onis, *m.*, the North wind, said to originate in Scythia

5. **nemus, -oris,** *n.*, grove, woods (she obviously has a very large peristylum!)

6. **satum:** *adj.*, sprung from, native to

    tecta: roof (SYNECDOCHE)

    remugiat: remugio, -ire, 4, resound, reply

7. **positas** (*p. part.*): **pono, -ere,** 3, place, put

    nives: nix, nivis, *f.*, snow

9. **pone** (*imperative*): as *depone*, put aside

10. **funis, -is,** *m.*, rope, cable. This reference is to an unspecified piece of machinery running backwards out of control when the rope has slipped.

11. **Penelopen** (*Greek acc.*): a reference to the patient wife of Odysseus, noted for turning away would-be suitors

procis: procus, -i, *m.*, suitor (dative of reference)

12. **Tyrrhenus:** Tuscany, the region north of Rome; originally in reference to Etruscans, a ruling class during the period of the Roman monarchy

13. **neque...nec...nec...:** the ANAPHORA emphasizes the increasing importance of the items listed

    preces: prayers

14. Some scholars (viz.: Bennett) suggest that the yellow, not the purple **viola** is referenced here, which works well with **pallor**

15. **Pieria:** a mountain in Thessaly

    paelice: *from* **paellex, paellicis,** *f.*, mistress

    saucius: *adj.*, wounded, stricken, afflicted

    The CHIASMUS of the stricken husband around his Pierian mistress is no doubt intended to goad Lyce into retaliating against his infidelity by establishing a relationship with the Poet.

16. **curvat:** bends (its object is **te** in 13)

17. **aesculo: aesculus, -i,** *f.*, a type of oak (noted for being unyielding)

18. **Mauris:** African, *from* **Maurus, -a, -um,** Mauritanian

    mitior: *comp. of* **mitis, -e,** soft, mild

    anguibus: anguis, -is, *m. or f.*, snake or serpent

19. **hoc:** (*with* **latus**) hence, "this body"

    liminis: limen, liminis, *n.*, threshold

20. **latus, lateris,** *n.*, side, flank; here, *by* METONYMY, body

HORACE *ODES* 3.10

Extremum Tanain si biberes, Lyce,
saevo nupta viro, me tamen asperas
porrectum ante fores obicere incolis
    plorares Aquilonibus.

audis quo strepitu ianua, quo nemus   5
inter pulchra satum tecta remugiat
ventis, et positas ut glaciet nives
    puro numine Iuppiter?

ingratam Veneri pone superbiam,
ne currente retro funis eat rota.   10
non te Penelopen difficilem procis
    Tyrrhenus genuit parens.

o quamvis neque te munera nec preces
nec tinctus viola pallor amantium
nec vir Pieria paelice saucius   15
    curvat, supplicibus tuis

parcas, nec rigida mollior aesculo
nec Mauris animum mitior anguibus.
non hoc semper erit liminis aut aquae
    caelestis patiens latus.   20

HORACE *ODES* 3.26: NOTES

Meter: Alcaic

We can see an echo of this poem in *Amores*, 3.15, by Ovid. The parallels are quite striking in so far as both poems create the METAPHOR of love as a war from which the poet is retiring and "hanging up his weapons" with a dedication or invocation to Venus.

1. **vixi: vivo, vivere,** 3, live
    puellis (*dat. of reference*)

2. **non sine:** LITOTES
    militavi: milito, 1, serve as a soldier

3. **defunctum: defungor, -i,** 3, *dep.*, be done with

4. **barbiton** (*Greek acc.*): the lyre

5. **laevum: laevus, -a, -um,** *adj.*, left

7. **funalia: funalis, -e,** *adj.*, here, wax torches
    vectes: vectis, -is, *m.*, lever or crowbar
    *The poet is hanging up all his weapons, from the lyre with which he serenaded his lady to the crowbars used to break down her door (hopefully, figuratively speaking)

8. **minaces: minax, -acis,** *adj.*, projecting, threatening (note CHIASMUS)

9. **diva, -ae,** *f.*, goddess
    Cyprum: Cyprus, traditionally an island dear to seaborn Venus

10. **Memphin** (*Greek acc.*): an Egyptian city where there was a shrine to Venus
    Sithonia: *adj.*, Thracian

11. **sublimi: sublimis, -e,** raised, lifted (abl. of means)
    flagello: flagellum, -i, *n.*, a whip or scourge

12. **semel,** *adv.*, once, a single time

HORACE ODES 3.26

Vixi puellis nuper idoneus
et militavi non sine gloria;
    nunc arma defunctumque bello
        barbiton hic paries habebit,

laevum marinae qui Veneris latus   5
custodit. hic, hic ponite lucida
    funalia et vectes et arcus*
        oppositis foribus minaces.

o quae beatam diva tenes Cyprum et
Memphin carentem Sithonia nive,   10
    regina, sublimi flagello
        tange Chloen semel arrogantem.

*in some MSS. this is *securesque*

HORACE *ODES* 4.11: NOTES

Meter: Sapphic & Adonic

In this charming poem, preparations are underway for a birthday celebration in honor of Maecenas, Horace's patron. As the poem begins, the poet is welcoming his guest Phyllis, telling her of the wine, pointing out where she might find parsley and ivy for her hair. He then seems to speak almost in an aside to Phyllis, mentioning that Telephus, a young man with whom she is in love, has moved on to a new girl—but he encourages Phyllis to forget about it and be joyful. Note the tender way that the poet refers to Phyllis in lines 30–31.

1. **est mihi...:** dat. of possession

    superantis (*pres. part.*): **supero,** here, surpassing or exceeding

2. **Albani:** METONYMY for wine; Alban wine was considered quite good, from the Alban hills in Latium.

    cadus, -i, *m.*, a large wine jar

    Note the word framing: **nonum** and **annum** around **superantes** and **plenus... cadus** containing the **Albani.**

3. **nectendis** (*gerundive*): dat. of purpose, "for weaving of crowns"

    Phylli: Greek vocative

4. **vis:** here, "a large amount, an abundance"

    hederae: ivy

5. **religata: religo,** 1, tie out of the way, bind back

    fulges: fulgeo, -ere, fulsi, shine forth, gleam

6. **ridet:** here, "looks bright or gleams"; you could translate **ridet** as "laughs," creating a PERSONIFICATION—the house laughing

    castis: castus, -a, -um, *adj.*, pure, holy

7. **vincta: vincio,** 2, bend, tie around, surround

    verbenis: verbena, -ae, *f.*, sacred boughs

8. **spargier:** archaic poetic form for the passive inf. *spargi*

9. **manus, -us,** *f.*, hand, *pl.* band or group; here a collective singular implying the household staff

10. **pueris** (*abl. of accomp.*): with **mixtae**

    cursitant: frequentive of **curso,** "running up and down"

11. **trepidant:** quiver, tremble

12. **vertice: vertex, verticis,** *m.*, at the top of; that which turns, whirls

    fumum: fumus, -i, *m.*, smoke

13. **noris:** syncopated perfect of *noveris*

14. **agendae:** with **sunt** (*passive periphrastic*): here, must be explained (**tibi**) to you

16. **findit: findo,** 3, divide, split, divide in half

17. **iure,** *adv.*, deservedly, rightly

18. **proprio,** *adj.*, my own

19. **adfluentes:** on-flowing

20. **ordinat:** sets in order

21. Note the word order: **Telephum** (whom you are after), then go to the end of the next line for **puella,** the subject of **occupavit.**

22. The parenthetical **non tuae sortis** (genitive of quality) assures her that her **iuvenem** is "not your kind."

24. **compede: compes, compedis,** *f.*, shackle, foot iron (like leg irons); an OXYMORON, since it is paired with **grata**

25. **ambustus** (p. part. from *amburo*): burned

    Phaethon: son of Apollo who begged to drive his father's sky chariot and flew too near the sun

    avaras, *adj.*, greedy, desirous

26. **ales, alitis,** *adj.*, winged

27. **gravatus, -a, -um,** *adj.*, weighed down (note CHIASMUS in "weighed-down Pegasus" with his "earth-bound rider" in the middle)

28. **Bellerophontem:** After he killed the Chimaera, proud Bellerophon attempted to ride Pegasus right up to Mt. Olympus, but the winged horse threw him.

Horace *Odes* 4.11

Est mihi nonum superantis annum
plenus Albani cadus; est in horto,
Phylli, nectendis apium coronis;
    est hederae vis

multa, qua crinis religata fulges;   5
ridet argento domus; ara castis
vincta verbenis avet immolato
    spargier agno;

cuncta festinat manus, huc et illuc
cursitant mixtae pueris puellae;   10
sordidum flammae trepidant rotantes
    vertice fumum.

ut tamen noris quibus advoceris
gaudiis, Idus tibi sunt agendae,
qui dies mensem Veneris marinae   15
    findit Aprilem,

iure sollemnis mihi sanctiorque
paene natali proprio, quod ex hac
luce Maecenas meus adfluentis
    ordinat annos.   20

Telephum, quem tu petis, occupavit
non tuae sortis iuvenem puella
dives et lasciva tenetque grata
    compede vinctum.

terret ambustus Phaethon avaras   25
spes, et exemplum grave praebet ales
Pegasus terrenum equitem gravatus
    Bellerophontem,

30. **quam licet** (*with* **ultra**): more than it is
    allowed

    nefas: *indecl.,* that which is against divine
    law

31. **disparem: dispar, disparis,** *adj.,* unequal,
    unlike; here, used as a substantive

33. **calebo: caleo,** 2, be in love with

34. **condisce: condisco,** 3, learn thoroughly

    modos: here, "rhythm, meter" (although,
    interestingly, it can also mean "modera-
    tion" or "to one's limits")

    The poet assures Phyllis that a song will
    diminish her dark cares.

semper ut te digna sequare et ultra
quam licet sperare nefas putando 30
disparem vites. age iam, meorum
    finis amorum—

non enim posthac alia calebo
femina—condisce modos, amanda
voce quos reddas: minuentur atrae 35
    carmine curae.

OVID

Cupids as wine merchants, House of the Vetii, Pompeii.
Photograph by Raymond V. Schroder, S. J.

OVID

Publius Ovidius Naso was born on March 20, 43 BC, in Sulmo, east of Rome in the Apennines. He also studied in Rome and Athens, although, unlike Horace, he was of a wealthy upper-class family. He turned down an appointment to the senate in order to pursue his passion for poetry. Acquainted with Horace, he became friends with Propertius and Tibullus. In his *Amores* he followed the models of Catullus, Tibullus, and Propertius, telling the story of his affection for a woman whom he named "Corinna." His copious works include *Heroides, Ars Amatoria, Remedia Amoris, Medicamina Faciei Femineae, Fasti, Metamorphoses, Tristia,* and *Epistulae ex Ponto.* The last four of these works were composed in exile (although *Metamorphoses* had been released at the very beginning of this time). According to historians, it would seem that Augustus felt that Ovid had committed some error of judgment with his poetry, and for this, he was banished for the remainder of his life to Tomis, on the Black Sea. Augustus was known to be sensitive to anything that denigrated "family values." Some biographers maintained that he even banished his daughter Julia for participating in the parties and poetry readings celebrating "The Art of Loving."

Ovid *Amores* 1.1: Notes

Meter: Elegiac Couplet

Ovid gives the impression in this, the first of his *Amores*, that he is beginning a grand epic in the manner of Virgil's *Arma virumque cano*.... Instead, as our poet goes on, Cupid intervenes and laughingly steals one foot from the second line in each pair. Epic verse cannot be accomplished in elegiacs, so the poet must write love poetry, having been hit by the god of love himself. The poet does not intend or want to write love poetry; he tries to beg off, but he is forced to do so by Cupid. Unlike Horace, who was asked by Maecenas in *Ode* 2.12 to write about war when the poet preferred love, Ovid has a god compelling him and cannot say no.

1. **bellum, -i,** *n.,* war

2. **edere: edo, edere, edidi, editus,** 3, put forth, publish

   modis: modus, -i, *m.,* measure, rhythm, melody

3. **inferior:** lower, subsequent; here, the five-foot line in elegiac couplet

   Cupido, Cupidinis, *m.,* Cupid

5. **"Quis tibi, saeve puer,...?":** The poet addresses Cupid here with the disdain used by Apollo in *Met.* 1.456: **Quid... tibi, lascive puer...?** Both males used the same complaint against the "boy" god: to stop meddling in their business. Apollo and the poet are both shot by Cupid, forthwith.

6. **Pieridum** (*patronymic*): of Pieria, Macedonia; i.e., of the Muses

   vates, -is, *m.,* seer, prophet, bard

7. **flavae: flavus, -a, -um,** *adj.,* blonde, yellow (descriptive epithet of Minerva)

8. **ventilet: ventilo,** 1, kindle, fan

   faces: fax, facis, *f.,* torch

   accensas . . . faces: flames, perhaps of desire or a reference to marriage customs, representative of Venus (chiasmus around **Minerva**)

9. **probet: probo,** 1, approve, esteem good

   iugosis: iugosus, -a, -um, *adj.,* mountainous

   Cererem: Ceres, goddess of grain, would normally have nothing to do with either woods or mountains

10. **pharetratae:** wearing a quiver; the *pharetrata virgo* (epithet) is Diana, goddess of the hunt

     arva coli: pass. inf., "fields to be cultivated by..."

11. **crinibus: crinis, -is,** *m.,* hair

11–12. **acuta cuspide** and **Marte movente** are both ablative with **instruo,** which takes the ablative when it means "equip."

12. **Aoniam: Aonius, -a, -um,** *adj.,* from Aonia or Boeotia (where Mt. Helicon was, sacred to Apollo)

13–14. **puer . . . ambitiose:** vocative

15. **tempe:** valley (*Greek neuter plural*). The Helicon is a symbol of Apollo

18. **attenuat: attenuo,** 1, reduce, weaken

19–20. **materia...:** boys, and girls with long hair were obviously necessary material for love poetry: Ovid says he has neither.

     Longas . . . comas: accusative of respect

21. **questus eram** (*p.p.*), **queror,** *dep.,* complain

     pharetra: read as *ex* **pharetra**

     protinus, *adv.,* directly, immediately

22. **in exitium:** for destruction

     spicula: spiculum,-i, *n.,* arrow, point, sting

23. **lunavitque: luno,** 1, bend like a crescent moon

     sinuosum, *adj.,* bent, curved

24. **canas: cano, canere, cecini,** —, 3, sing

     Note the harsh sounds of *q, c, t,* and *x* in this line, as Cupid fires on the poet: the words must be ennunciated clearly as this is read aloud.

26. **uror,** *dep.:* burn

     The assonance in this line reflects the groaning of the wounded poet, contrasting with the harsh consonance of the archer in 24.

Ovid *Amores* 1.1

Arma gravi numero violentaque bella parabam
　　edere, materia conveniente modis.
par erat inferior versus; risisse Cupido
　　dicitur atque unum surripuisse pedem.
"quis tibi, saeve puer, dedit hoc in carmina iuris?　　　　5
　　Pieridum vates, non tua, turba sumus.
quid, si praeripiat flavae Venus arma Minervae,
　　ventilet accensas flava Minerva faces?
quis probet in silvis Cererem regnare iugosis,
　　lege pharetratae virginis arva coli?　　　　　　　　10
crinibus insignem quis acuta cuspide Phoebum
　　instruat, Aoniam Marte movente lyram?
sunt tibi magna, puer, nimiumque potentia regna:
　　cur opus adfectas, ambitiose, novum?
an, quod ubique, tuum est? tua sunt Heliconia tempe?　　15
　　vix etiam Phoebo iam lyra tuta sua est?
cum bene surrexit versu nova pagina primo,
　　attenuat nervos proximus ille meos.
nec mihi materia est numeris levioribus apta,
　　aut puer aut longas compta puella comas."　　　　　20
questus eram, pharetra cum protinus ille soluta
　　legit in exitium spicula facta meum
lunavitque genu sinuosum fortiter arcum
　　"quod" que "canas, vates, accipe" dixit "opus."
me miserum! certas habuit puer ille sagittas:　　　　　25
　　uror, et in vacuo pectore regnat Amor.

27. **surgat . . . residat:** iussive subjunctives

28. **ferrea . . . bella:** vocative

    ferrea: ferreus, -a, -um, *adj.,* iron; SYNECDO-CHE in this context

29. **flaventia: flavens, flaventis,** *adj.,* light yellow.

tempora: tempus, temporis, *n.:* esp. in pl. this word means "temples," as in "the side of the head"

30. **undenos: undeni, -ae, -a,** *pl. adj.,* lines of eleven feet each

    emodulanda: emodulor, *dep.,* celebrate (gerundive)

sex mihi surgat opus numeris, in quinque residat;
    ferrea cum vestris bella valete modis.
cingere litorea flaventia tempora myrto,
    Musa, per undenos emodulanda pedes.   30

Ovid *Amores* 1.3: Notes

Meter: Elegiac Couplet

    This poem reads like a prayer: note Ovid's opening words. The poet asks that his lady who has recently conquered his heart, love him, or at least allow herself to be loved. Asking Venus to hear his many prayers, he promises to reward her with immortality in song.

1. **iusta: iustus, -a, -um,** *adj.,* lawful, allowed, just

    praedata: *from* **praedor,** *dep.,* take booty, plunder

3. **A,** *interj.,* Ah!

    patiatur: *from* **patior** (*dep.*), suffer, bear, endure

4. **Cytherea:** Venus, who was said by Hesiod to have risen from the sea near the island of Cythera

5. **deserviat: deservio,** 4, serve zealously

6. **norit:** *syncopation of* **noverit,** *from* **nosco, -ere, novi, notus,** 3, learn

7. **commendant: commendo,** 1, recommend, entrust

9. **renovatur: renovo,** 1, renew, restore

    aratris: aratrum, -i, *n.,* plow

10. **parcus: parcus, -a, -um,** *adj.,* frugal, thrifty

11. **at,** *conj.,* but

    Having admitted his faults, Ovid lists his reasons for deserving Venus' help.

    Phoebus comitesque novem: Apollo and the nine Muses, goddesses of the arts.

    novem: *indecl.,* nine

    vitis, -is, *f.,* grapevine

    repertor: discoverer, i.e. Bacchus (god of wine), hence, discoverer of the vine

12. **hac faciunt:** Phoebus, the Muses, Bacchus, Cupid, **fides, mores, simplicitas,** and **pudor:** they all do (or act in) this (**hac**)

    Amor: both Cupid, god of love, and love itself (**amor** with a small *a*)

13. **cessura: cedo,** 3, *fut. part.,* yield, give way

14. **purpureusque:** purple; referring to **pudor,** can mean blushing or beautiful. Best taken with both senses.

15. **mihi:** dative with **placeo**

    Note 15–19: ANAPHORA with **mihi**

    desultor, desultoris, *m.,* one who is inconstant, one who "jumps around" from one to another

16. **qua:** in any way; supply *est*

17. **fila: filum, -i,** *n.,* threads. The sisters here are the Fates, who weave the threads of human lives.

21. **nomen:** name, i.e., renown

    exterrita (*p.p.*)**: exterreo,** 2, frighten

    Io: one of Zeus' lovers; he transformed her into a cow so that Hera would not discover his infidelity.

22. **fluminea: flumineus, -a, -um,** *adj.,* of a river (abl. of description)

    lusit: ludo, 3, play

    adulter, -i, *m.,* one who is adulterous, unchaste. Another reference to Zeus, who assumed the form of a swan to seduce Leda, mother of Helen, Clytemnestra, and the Dioscuri

23. **simulato** (*p.p.*)**: simulo,** 1, imitate, take the form of

    iuvenco: iuvencus, -i, *m.,* young bull. Zeus took on the guise of a bull to successfully entice Europa.

24. **vara: varus, -a, -um,** *adj.,* crooked, bent

OVID *AMORES* 1.3

Iusta precor: quae me nuper praedata puella est
  aut amet aut faciat cur ego semper amem.
a, nimium volui: tantum patiatur amari;
  audierit nostras tot Cytherea preces.
accipe, per longos tibi qui deserviat annos;   5
  accipe, qui pura norit amare fide.
si me non veterum commendant magna parentum
  nomina, si nostri sanguinis auctor eques,
nec meus innumeris renovatur campus aratris,
  temperat et sumptus parcus uterque parens: 10
at Phoebus comitesque novem vitisque repertor
  hac faciunt et me qui tibi donat Amor
et nulli cessura fides, sine crimine mores,
  nudaque simplicitas purpureusque pudor.
non mihi mille placent, non sum desultor amoris: 15
  tu mihi, si qua fides, cura perennis eris;
tecum, quos dederint annos mihi fila sororum,
  vivere contingat teque dolente mori;
te mihi materiem felicem in carmina praebe:
  provenient causa carmina digna sua.   20
carmine nomen habent exterrita cornibus Io
  et quam fluminea lusit adulter ave
quaeque super pontum simulato vecta iuvenco
  virginea tenuit cornua vara manu.
nos quoque per totum pariter cantabimur orbem   25
  iunctaque semper erunt nomina nostra tuis.

OVID *AMORES* 1.9: NOTES

Meter: Elegiac Couplet

In this poem, Ovid compares for his friend Atticus the traits and attributes of soldiers and lovers, emphasizing his theme that all lovers are soldiers. Both types of men must be young and strong, they must camp on the cold ground, climb mountains, ford raging rivers and endure all that the harsh elements present to them for their conquest in this "war."

3. **habilis, -e,** *adj.,* fit, apt (+ dat.)
   convenit: convenio, 4, be fit, suitable

4. **turpe senex miles:** supply *est*
   turpe: turpis, -e, *adj.,* disgusting, shameful

5. **petiere = petiverunt**

7. **pervigilant: pervigilo,** 1, watch all night
   ambo: both

10. **exempto fine:** ablative absolute
    exempto: eximo, 3, take away, remove
    fine: finis, -is, *m.,* boundary

11. **duplicataque: duplicatusque, -aque, umque,** *adj.,* doubled
    nimbo: nimbus, -i, *m.,* rainstorm

12. **congestas: congero,** 3, collect, heap up
    exteret: extero, 3, tread upon, crush
    nives: nix, nivis, *f.,* snow

13. **freta pressurus:** about to sail the sea
    freta: fretum, -i, *n.,* straits, sea
    tumidos: tumidus, -a, -um, swollen with anger; here, with **Euros:** enraged East wind
    causabitur: causor, *dep.,* use as an excuse

14. **verrendis** (*gerundive*): **verro, -ere,** 3, sweep (i.e., sail)
    Note interlocked word order

16. Golden line (two adjectives and two nouns with a verb between them)
    perfero: here, "endure, withstand"
    imbre: imber, -is, *m.,* heavy rain

17. **speculator, -oris,** *m.,* scout, spy

20. **obsidet: obsideo,** 2, to beset, blockade, besiege
    portas ... fores: "gates ... doors"; the former is the objective of the soldier, the latter, of the lover
    frangit: frango, 3, dash, break

21. **soporatos: soporatus, -a, -um,** *adj.,* asleep, stupefied
    profuit: *from* **prosum:** benefit, profit (impersonal)

22. **inerme: inermis, -e,** *adj.,* unarmed, helpless

23. Golden line
    Threicii: Threicius, -a, -um, *adj.,* Thracian, of Thrace, a region east of Macedon in Greece
    Rhesi: Rhesus, a leader of the Thracians and ally of Troy in the Trojan War.
    Homer relates in Book 10 of the *Iliad* how the Greek heroes Diomedes and Odysseus made a foray by night into the Thracian camp, killed Rhesus and some of his companions, and stole his horses. Ironically, Ovid, from the outset of the *Amores,* wanted to write epic poetry in the manner of Homer, but was prevented by Cupid

24. **capti ... equi:** vocative. The stolen horses of Rhesus are APOSTROPHIZED.

25. **nempe,** *conj.,* certainly, without doubt
    somnis: ablative with **utor**
    utuntur: utor, *dep.,* use, profit from

26. **arma:** strong sexual connotations, employing the parallels between lover and soldier. Each has his own weaponry.
    sopitis hostibus: ablative absolute

27. **manus:** normally "hand," but here meaning "group" or "band"
    catervas: caterva, -ae, *f.,* crowd, throng

30. **iacere: iaceo,** 2, lie down, be prostrate

31. **quicumque:** whosoever

32. **desinat: desino,** 3, cease, desist (iussive subjunctive)
    ingenii...experientis: descriptive genitives

OVID *AMORES* 1.9

Militat omnis amans, et habet sua castra Cupido;
　　Attice, crede mihi, militat omnis amans.
quae bello est habilis, Veneri quoque convenit aetas:
　　turpe senex miles, turpe senilis amor.
quos petiere duces animos* in milite forti,　　　　　　　5
　　hos petit in socio bella puella viro:
pervigilant ambo, terra requiescit uterque;
　　ille fores dominae servat, at ille ducis.
militis officium longa est via: mitte puellam,
　　strenuus exempto fine sequetur amans;　　　　　　10
ibit in adversos montes duplicataque nimbo
　　flumina, congestas exteret ille nives,
nec freta pressurus tumidos causabitur Euros
　　aptaque verrendis sidera quaeret aquis.
quis nisi vel miles vel amans et frigora noctis　　　　　15
　　et denso mixtas perferet imbre nives?
mittitur infestos alter speculator in hostes,
　　in rivale oculos alter, ut hoste, tenet.
ille graves urbes, hic durae limen amicae
　　obsidet; hic portas frangit, at ille fores.　　　　　　20
saepe soporatos invadere profuit hostes
　　caedere et armata vulgus inerme manu;
sic fera Threicii ceciderunt agmina Rhesi,
　　et dominum capti deseruistis equi:
nempe maritorum somnis utuntur amantes　　　　　25
　　et sua sopitis hostibus arma movent.
custodum transire manus vigilumque catervas
　　militis et miseri semper amantis opus.
Mars dubius, nec certa Venus: victique resurgunt,
　　quosque neges umquam posse iacere, cadunt.　　30
ergo desidiam quicumque vocabat amorem,
　　desinat: ingenii est experientis Amor.

---

*annos in some mss.

33. **Briseide** (*abl.*): Briseis, the woman who had been taken as a slave by Achilles, and for whom he sulked throughout much of the *Iliad*, when Agamemnon took her from him.

    maestus, -a, -um, *adj.,* sad, full of sorrow

34. **frangite, Troes** (*voc.*): Ovid is advising the Trojans long after the fact, thereby creating this APOSTROPHE

    Argeas: Argeus, -a, -um, *adj.,* Argive, describing someone or something from Greece

    opes: ops, opis, *f.,* here, strengths or resources (defense works)

35. Hector's leaving his wife and child to go back to the war is a scene poignantly rendered in Book 6 of the *Iliad*; Ovid's point here is that it was his wife Andromache who "put the helmet on his head," sending him back to the battle to save them all.

    Andromache, Andromaches, *f.:* the wife of Hector

    conplexibus = complexibus. *N.B.:* the Latin text is printed according to the Oxford edition, as are IB exams, but many dictionaries and some texts convert *con-* to *com-*

36. **galeam: galea, -ae,** *f.,* helmet

37. **Atrides:** patronymic for Agamemnon, son of Atreus.

    Priameide: patronymic for Cassandra, daughter of Priam, king of Troy

    fertur: it is said

38. **Maenadis:** the frenzied followers of Bacchus, who were in the habit of roaming the countryside and tearing things apart. Their hair was often disheveled; note the hissing of the *s* repetition in this line.

    effusis: effusus, -a, -um, *adj.,* poured out, flowing; "disheveled" with **comis**

    obstipuisse: obstipesco, obstupesco, 3, be astounded, stupefied

39. Ovid here makes a reference to the story of Vulcan, husband of Venus, engineering the capture, in a bronze net, of his wife and her lover Mars *in flagrante delicto*

    deprensus (*p.p.*): **deprendo, 3,** seized, caught

    fabrilia: fabrilis, -e, *adj.,* of the craftsman (specifically Vulcan in this case)

    vincula: vinculum, -i, *n.,* rope, binding

40. **notior** (*comp.*): **notus, -a, -um,** *adj.,* known

41. **segnis, -e,** *adj.,* slow, slack

    discinctaque: discinctus, -a, -um, *adj.,* ungirt, without a girdle, therefore dissolute

43. **formosae: formosus, -a, -um,** *adj.,* beautiful

    cura (+ *gen.*): "love or caring for"; also, "military concern/responsibility"

    inpulet = impulit (*see note 35*), from **impello, 3,** to strike, drive against, set in motion

44. **aera: aes, aeris,** *n.,* metal, copper, bronze; hence, money, salary

46. **desidiosus, -a, -um,** *adj.,* slothful, indolent

ardet in abducta Briseide maestus Achilles
    (dum licet, Argeas frangite, Troes, opes);
Hector ab Andromaches conplexibus ibat ad arma,   35
    et galeam capiti quae daret, uxor erat;
summa ducum, Atrides visa Priameide fertur
    Maenadis effusis obstipuisse comis;
Mars quoque deprensus fabrilia vincula sensit:
    notior in caelo fabula nulla fuit.   40
ipse ego segnis eram discinctaque in otia natus;
    mollierant animos lectus et umbra meos;
inpulit ignavum formosae cura puellae,
    iussit et in castris aera merere suis.
inde vides agilem nocturnaque bella gerentem: 45
    qui nolet fieri desidiosus, amet.

OVID *AMORES* 1.11: NOTES

Meter: Elegiac Couplet

     In this poem, Ovid is employing a go-between, a serving girl named Nape, to carry a tablet to his love Corinna. He praises the girl's cleverness, invoking her to watch her mistress carefully as she reads, to report to the poet every subtle expression on her face, and then to bring back her message quickly!

1. **colligere: colligo,** 3, gather, collect

   incertos . . . crines: object of both **colligere** and **ponere**

2. **ancillas inter:** ANASTROPHE

   habenda: the sense is not "to be had" but "to be considered"

   Nape: the serving girl, intermediary between the poet and the lady

4. **dandis** (*gerundive*): **do,** 1, give

5. **hortata: hortor,** *dep.,* urge (supply *es* for the best reading)

6. **laboranti: laboro,** 1, troubled

7. **peraratas: peraro,** 1, plough through; write, inscribe

   mane, *adv.,* early in the morning

8. **sedula: sedulus, -a, -um,** *adj.,* persistent, diligent

   pelle: pello, 3, strike, beat

   moras: mora, -ae, *f.,* delay

   obstantes: pres. part. of **obsto,** 1, stand in the way of, obstruct

9. **silicum: silex, -icis,** *m.,* stone

   venae: vena, -ae, *f.,* vein, streak

11. **credibile est:** "it is believable that . . ."

    arcus: arcus, -us, *m.,* bow

12. **militiae: militia, -ae,** *f.,* military service, warfare

    signa: "standards," as those carried by Roman soldiers

    tuere: tueor, *dep.,* watch over, defend, guard

13. **quaeret: quaero,** 3, seek

    quid agam: "how I am doing"

14. **cera, -ae,** *f.,* wax; the message is carved on a wax tablet

    notata: known, marked

15. **vacuae:** here, translate not as "empty" but rather as "idle"; it modifies **dominae,** which is implied

16. **continuo,** *adv.,* straightway, immediately

17. **mando,** 1, give over, entrust, request (add "that")

19. **perlectis: perlego,** 3, examine thoroughly. One-word ablative absolute with the tablets implied as those which are examined

20. **late,** *adv.,* widely

21. **comprimat: comprimo,** 3, compress, squeeze tightly (hortatory subjunctive)

22. **margine: margo, -inis,** *m.,* edge, border, margin

    rasa: rado, 3, rub, smooth; but here: inscribe

23. **digitos: digitus, -i,** *m.,* finger

    opus est (*idiom*): "it is necessary"

    graphio: graphium, -i, *n.,* pen, stylus

    lassare: lasso, 1, tire, make weary

25. **victrices: victrix, -icis,** *adj.,* reporting a victory, victorious. The *tabellae* are personified as returning from battle to a triumph, wreathed with the traditional laurel.

    redimire: redimio, 4, encircle, gird

26. **aede: aedes, -is,** *f.,* temple, sanctuary

28. **nuper,** *adv.,* recently

    vile: vilis, -e, *adj.,* cheap

    acer, -eris, *n.,* maple wood

OVID *AMORES* 1.11

Colligere incertos et in ordine ponere crines
    docta neque ancillas inter habenda Nape
inque ministeriis furtivae cognita noctis
    utilis et dandis ingeniosa notis,
saepe venire ad me dubitantem hortata Corinnam,   5
    saepe laboranti fida reperta mihi,
accipe et ad dominam peraratas mane tabellas
    perfer et obstantes sedula pelle moras.
nec silicum venae nec durum in pectore ferrum
    nec tibi simplicitas ordine maior adest;   10
credibile est et te sensisse Cupidinis arcus;
    in me militiae signa tuere tuae.
si quaeret quid agam, spe noctis vivere dices;
    cetera fert blanda cera notata manu.
dum loquor, hora fugit: vacuae bene redde tabellas,   15
    verum continuo fac tamen illa legat.
aspicias oculos mando frontemque legentis:
    et tacito vultu scire futura licet.
nec mora, perlectis rescribat multa iubeto:
    odi, cum late splendida cera vacat.   20
comprimat ordinibus versus, oculosque moretur
    margine in extremo littera rasa meos.
quid digitos opus est graphio lassare tenendo?
    hoc habeat scriptum tota tabella "veni."
non ego victrices lauro redimire tabellas   25
    nec Veneris media ponere in aede morer.
subscribam VENERI FIDAS SIBI NASO MINISTRAS
    DEDICAT. AT NUPER VILE FUISTIS ACER.

OVID *AMORES* 1.12: NOTES

Meter: Elegiac Couplet

This poem is the sad conclusion to the story of the tablets in *Amores* 1.11. Here, the message has been returned—and it is bad, for our poet. The tablets which only one poem earlier he was thinking of hanging in a sacred shrine, he now curses vehemently. Nape is diminished in the poet's eyes as being clumsy; in addition he curses the tablets and the tree from which they were made, the wax, and the comb from which it was gathered!

1. **Flete: fleo,** 2, Weep! (We know from the first word that the news is bad.)

   rediere = **redierunt**

2. **infelix, -icis,** *adj.,* unhappy, unproductive, ill-omened

3. **omina: omen, ominis,** *n.,* omen, sign

4. **Nape, Napes,** *f.,* Nape, the serving girl from Poem 1.11

   restitit: restito, 1, linger, loiter

   icta: ico, -ere, ici, ictus, 3, strike, smite

   Tripping over a threshold was very bad luck in Rome, which is why brides are carried over theirs.

5. **memento: memini, -isse,** *def.,* remember

6. **cautius** (*comp.*): **caute,** *adv.,* careful, cautious

   sobria: sobrius, -a, -um, *adj.,* sober, careful

7. **funebria: funebris, -e,** *adj.,* funereal (voc. pl.)

8. **negaturis: nego,** 1, refuse (fut. part.)

   referta, *adj.:* crowded, bursting with

   nota, -ae, *f.,* letters, words, marks

   Note the CHIASMUS around the crowded wax.

9. **cicutae:** hemlock (used as a poison)

10. **infamis, -e,** *adj.,* notorious, disreputable

    apis, -is, *f.,* bee

11. **minio: minium, -i,** *n.,* cinnabar (a red dye and medicinal agent)

    rubebas: rubeo, 2, to be red, blush

    medicata: medicatus, -a, -um, *adj.* (from **medico**), medicated, drugged, or (here) dyed

12. **sanguinulentus, -a, -um,** *adj.,* bloody

13. **proiectae** (*voc.*): referring to the *tabellae,* those which are thrown out

    triviis: trivium, -i, *n.,* crossroads

    iaceatis: iacio, 3 (iussive subjunctive)

    inutile: inutilis, -e, *adj.,* useless

14. **rota, -ae,** *f.,* wheel (SYNECDOCHE)

    praetereuntis: praetereo, 4, go by, pass by

16. **convincam: convinco,** 3, here, prove, assure

17. **suspendia: suspendium, -i,** *n.,* hanging (as form of execution)

    collo: collum, -i, *n.,* neck (by which one would be hanged)

18. **carnifici: carnifex, -icis,** *m.,* executioner, hangman

    cruces: crux, crucis, *f.,* cross

19. **raucis: raucus, -a, -um,** *adj.,* hoarse

    bubonibus: bubo, -onis, *m.,* horned owl

20. **volturis: voltur, -uris,** *m.,* vulture

    strix, -igis, *f.,* screech-owl

23. **vadimonia: vadimonium, -i,** *n.,* bail-bond, security (Ovid feels that the tablets are more suited for wordy legal documents than as he had used them: for loving words!)

    garrula: garrulus, -a, -um, *adj.,* chattering, prattling, talkative

24. **cognitor, -oris,** *m.,* advocate, attorney

25. **ephemeridas: ephemeris, -idis, -idas** (*acc. pl.*), *f.,* day-book, diary

26. **avarus, -a, -um,** *adj.,* greedy, grasping

27. **duplices: duplex, -icis,** *adj.,* double, and hence two-faced. Ovid's *tabellae* were both double tablets and back-stabbing allies, as their name suggests (**pro nomine**)

28. **auspicii...boni:** descriptive genitive

29. **precer: precor,** *dep.,* ask, beg, supplicate (deliberative subjunctive)

    cariosa: cariosus, -a, -um, *adj.,* dried up, decayed

30. **rodat: rodo,** 3, gnaw

    immundo: immundus, -a, -um, *adj.,* unclean, impure

    situs, -us, *m.,* neglect

OVID *AMORES* 1.12

Flete meos casus: tristes rediere tabellae;
    infelix hodie littera posse negat.
omina sunt aliquid: modo cum discedere vellet,
    ad limen digitos restitit icta Nape.
missa foras iterum limen transire memento   5
    cautius atque alte sobria ferre pedem.
ite hinc, difficiles, funebria ligna, tabellae,
    tuque, negaturis cera referta notis,
quam, puto, de longae collectam flore cicutae
    melle sub infami Corsica misit apis.   10
at tamquam minio penitus medicata rubebas:
    ille color vere sanguinulentus erat.
proiectae triviis iaceatis, inutile lignum,
    vosque rotae frangat praetereuntis onus.
illum etiam, qui vos ex arbore vertit in usum,   15
    convincam puras non habuisse manus;
praebuit illa arbor misero suspendia collo,
    carnifici diras praebuit illa cruces;
illa dedit turpes raucis bubonibus umbras,
    volturis in ramis et strigis ova tulit.   20
his ego commisi nostros insanus amores
    molliaque ad dominam verba ferenda dedi?
aptius hae capiant vadimonia garrula cerae,
    quas aliquis duro cognitor ore legat;
inter ephemeridas melius tabulasque iacerent,   25
    in quibus absumptas fleret avarus opes.
ergo ego vos rebus duplices pro nomine sensi:
    auspicii numerus non erat ipse boni.
quid precer iratus, nisi vos cariosa senectus
    rodat, et inmundo cera sit alba situ?   30

OVID *AMORES* 3.15

Meter: Elegiac Couplet

In this, the last of Ovid's *Amores*, the poet begins with an APOSTROPHE to "the mother of tender loves," urging Venus to seek a new spokesman, since he is moving on. He rejoices in the fact that, even as Mantua has Virgil and Verona has Catullus, his Sulmo shall ever be immortalized because of him.

1. **tenerorum: tener, -a, -um,** *adj.,* tender, soft

2. **meta, -ae,** *f.,* turning-post, goal

   Note the CHIASMUS in this METAPHOR.

   raditur: rado, 3, move past closely, graze, touch upon

3. **Paeligni:** Ovid hailed from central Italy, home of the Paelignian tribe

   alumnus, -i, *m.,* nursling, foster son

4. **dedecuere: dedeceo,** 2, disgrace

   Note the LITOTES in this line.

5. **quid:** i.e., *aliquid*

   proavis: proavus, -i, *m.,* forefather (before one's grandfather)

   heres, heredis, m./c.: heir, successor

6. **turbine: turbo, turbinis,** *m.,* spinning object, such as a whirlwind

8. **dicar:** future passive

9. **libertas, libertatis,** *f.,* freedom, independence

10. A reference to Paeligni's role in the Social War (91–87 BC), in which the non-Roman towns of Italy rose up against Rome. Rome ended the war by making political concessions, including Roman citizenship to Italians south of the Po River.

    socias . . . manus surrounds **anxia Roma** in a vivid and appropriate CHIASMUS.

11. **Sulmonis: Sulmo, Sulmonis,** *m.,* Ovid's birthplace

12. **iugera: iugerum, -i,** *n.,* fields, acres

14. **quantulacumque:** "however small"

15. **culte puer** (*voc.*): from **colo, colere, colui, cultum,** cultivate, or (here) pay respect, worship; hence: "worshipful child..."

    Note the ANAPHORA.

    Amathusia: of Amathus, a town in Cyprus associated with Venus

16. A golden line containing the word "golden"

    vellite: vello, -ere, —, 3, pull, tear out

    His military image for this set of poems is completed by his "breaking camp" with this verse.

17. **corniger . . . Lyaeus:** the "horned Liberator" is Bacchus

    increpuit: increpo, 1, **-ui, -itus,** make a loud noise

    thyrso: a staff, entwined with ivy and grape vines, carried by Dionysus, and with which he inspired poets

18. **magnis area maior equis:** Ovid attempts to return to the lofty themes upon which he had hoped to write from the beginning. Large spaces and big horses are appropriate topics for epic poetry.

19. **inbelles: inbellis, -e,** *adj.,* not warlike, peaceful

20. **superstes, -itis,** *adj.,* outliving, surviving

    opus: work; THE work, his *Amores*, are now complete with this last word.

OVID *AMORES* 3.15

Quaere novum vatem, tenerorum mater Amorum:
 raditur haec elegis ultima meta meis;
quos ego conposui, Paeligni ruris alumnus,
 (nec me deliciae dedecuere meae)
si quid id est, usque a proavis vetus ordinis heres,   5
 non modo militiae turbine factus eques.
Mantua Vergilio gaudet, Verona Catullo;
 Paelignae dicar gloria gentis ego,
quam sua libertas ad honesta coegerat arma,
 cum timuit socias anxia Roma manus.   10
atque aliquis spectans hospes Sulmonis aquosi
 moenia, quae campi iugera pauca tenent,
"quae tantum" dicet "potuistis ferre poetam,
 quantulacumque estis, vos ego magna voco."
culte puer puerique parens Amathusia culti,   15
 aurea de campo vellite signa meo;
corniger increpuit thyrso graviore Lyaeus:
 pulsanda est magnis area maior equis.
inbelles elegi, genialis Musa, valete,
 post mea mansurum fata superstes opus.   20

APPENDIX ONE

POETRY

Poetry is an expression of emotion through words. Not by coincidence does the Latin word for poet, *vates*, also mean "oracle" or "prophet": one who tells the future, who looks into the mind of the seeker and knows that person's thoughts, loves, and fears. The bond between a poet and his audience is a very personal one, for the writer's appeal is aimed directly at the heart of the listener. A poet's audience is a "listener," more than a "reader," because poetry, especially classical poetry, was created to be heard. Lyric poetry, like the lyrics to a song, was intended to be sung to the accompaniment of a lyre; there is a beat to classical poetry, called "meter," which establishes a constant rhythm throughout the poem.

The purpose of this small text is not to instruct in the fine points of Latin meter, but rather to present the works of three of the greatest poets in the Latin language for students of moderate experience in the reading of Latin. We shall merely describe, therefore, the patterns in metrical feet for each style presented by the authors under consideration. In brief, Latin meter is marked by long and short syllables, long designated by a '—' over the designated vowel, and short syllables by a '∪.' Some syllables can be either long or short; such syllable is called an "anceps" and marked with an '×.' A syllable is long if it contains a naturally long vowel (like the *a* in a first declension ablative, etc.), a diphthong (ae, oe, ei, ui, au, eu), or if the vowel is followed by two or more consonants. Metrical feet are made up of dactyls (— ∪ ∪), spondees (— —), iambs (∪ —), trochees (— ∪), and choriambs (— ∪ ∪ —).

POETIC METERS AND SCANSION

METERS OF CATULLUS

HENDECASYLLABIC

This is a lyric meter, deriving its name from the eleven syllables that comprise a line. These syllables are not marked off in feet, just rhythmic long and short combinations; for example:

— ∪ — ∪ ∪ — ∪ — ∪ — ×

(either of the first two syllables may be long or short)

LIMPING IAMBICS

This meter consists of six feet: five iambs (∪ —) and a trochee (— ∪) or spondee (— —). Spondees may be substituted in the first and third feet.

∪ — / ∪ — / ∪ — / ∪ — / ∪ — / — ×

(either the first or fifth syllable may be long)

SAPPHIC STROPHE

This form was named for Sappho, considered the prototypical lyric poet, and honored by both Catullus and Horace with poems written in her style. There are three identical lines followed by an Adonic, a closing line at the end of the stanza.

— ∪ — — — ∪ ∪ — ∪ — —

— ∪ — — — ∪ ∪ — ∪ — —

— ∪ — — — ∪ ∪ — ∪ — —

— ∪ ∪ — ×

(the fourth syllable may be short in the first three lines)

DACTYLIC HEXAMETERS

This is known as "epic meter," that in which the *Iliad, Odyssey,* and *Aeneid* were composed. Catullus uses this meter in Poem 62, and it is the meter Ovid says he intended to use when he had the elegiac couplet "forced" upon him by Cupid.

$$- \cup \cup / - \cup \cup / - \cup \cup / - \cup \cup / - \cup \cup / - \times$$

(any—or all—of the first four feet could be spondees; while the fifth foot is usually a dactyl, on occasion it is a spondee)

ELEGIAC COUPLET

This form, used also by Ovid throughout his *Amores*, consists of a dactylic hexameter line followed by a pentameter line; hence, Ovid complains in the first poem of his epic first line, and then Cupid's "stealing" one foot from the second line, making it a pentameter. Catullus uses this meter for all his poems after Poem 64. The scheme is thus:

$$- \cup \cup / - \cup \cup / - \cup \cup / - \cup \cup / - \cup \cup / - - \text{ (six metrical feet)}$$

(any or all of the first four feet may be a spondee, instead of a dactyl)

$$- \cup \cup / - \cup \cup / - // - \cup \cup / - \cup \cup / - \text{ (five metrical feet)}$$

(either or both of the first two feet may be spondees)

METERS OF HORACE

ALCAIC

This meter, often used in Horace's *Odes*, is named for Greek poet Alcaeus from Sappho's island, Lesbos.

$$\times - \cup - - // - \cup \cup - \cup \times$$

$$\times - \cup - - // - \cup \cup - \cup \times$$

$$\times - \cup - - - \cup - \times$$

$$- \cup \cup - \cup \cup - \cup - \times$$

SECOND ASCLEPIADEAN

This begins with a Glyconic line, a version of which is found in all Asclepiadean meters. Asclepiades was a Greek poet who revived Sapphic and Alcaic forms.

$$- - - \cup \cup - \cup \times$$

$$- - - \cup \cup - // - \cup \cup - \cup \times$$

THIRD ASCLEPIADEAN

$$– – – \cup\cup – // – \cup\cup – \cup\times$$

$$– – – \cup\cup – // – \cup\cup – \cup\times$$

$$– – – \cup\cup – // – \cup\cup – \cup\times$$

$$– – – \cup\cup – \cup\times$$

FOURTH ASCLEPIADEAN

$$– – – \cup\cup – //– \cup\cup – \cup\times$$

$$– – – \cup\cup – //– \cup\cup – \cup\times$$

$$– – – \cup\cup – \times$$

$$– – – \cup\cup – \cup\times$$

FIFTH ASCLEPIADEAN

$$– – – \cup\cup – // – \cup\cup – // – \cup\cup – \cup\times$$

SAPPHIC

(discussed above, in Catullan meter)

METERS OF OVID

In his *Amores,* included in this text, Ovid used only Elegiac Couplet, discussed above, in Meters of Catullus.

APPENDIX TWO

RHETORICAL / LITERARY FIGURES

Rhetorical / literary figures are the pigments with which a poet paints the vivid pictures characteristic of his or her craft. They allow the reader to form mental images, so that the reader and the poet are walking together in a shared literary experience. Since poetry is generally more evocative of emotion than prose, these figures are important vehicles for imagery, emotion, and enhanced meaning.

ALLEGORY: a representation of a spiritual or abstract concept through the use of a story, which is easier to visualize; an extended METAPHOR. Ovid uses war as an allegorical representation of love and the "battles" a lover must "fight" to win the object of his love.

ALLITERATION: the repetition of initial sounds (generally consonantal) in a series of words, as in Catullus 5: *senum severiorum* (2), *aestimemus assis* (3), and *milia multa* (10).

ANAPHORA: the repetition of an initial word in several succeeding phrases, clauses, or sentences. This can be illustrated in the same poem by Catullus 5, lines 7–10: *...deinde centum, dein...dein...deinde...deinde centum. Dein...*

ANTITHESIS: placing two obviously opposing ideas or concepts side by side for rhetorical effect, as in Catullus' *odi et amo* or in his Poem 62, lines 42 and 44 with the boys' vs. girls' version of the wedding night.

APOSTROPHE: an emotional address to some person or thing not present, as Ovid does in *Amores* 3.15, line 1: *Quaere novum vatem, tenerorum mater Amorum...*

ASSONANCE: the repetition of sounds in words of close proximity, as in Catullus 45, lines 3 and 4, and again in line 20: *...amo atque amare...assidue...paratus annos...* and *animis amant amantur.*

ASYNDETON: the omission of conjunctions in sentences or groups of phrases or words where they would normally be expected. In *Amores* 3.15, Ovid notes that *Mantua Vergilio gaudet, Verona Catullo...*

CHIASMUS: the arrangement of words in reversed or opposite patterns (ABBA), for example, by parts of speech as "noun adj. adj. noun" or "verb noun noun verb," or by cases as "nom. gen. gen. nom.," in framed elements, as found in Horace *Ode* 1.22: *Integer vitae scelerisque purus...*

CONSONANCE: The correspondence of consonants, especially at the ends of words, as opposed to ASSONANCE, which is usually applied to vowel sounds only.

ELLIPSIS: the omission of a word or words that can nonetheless be gained from context; quite often this is a form of *sum* that should be placed with a participle, or just inserted for meaning, as illustrated in Horace, *Ode* 1.5, line 12: *miseri (sunt)...*

ENJAMBMENT: an overflow of a phrase onto the next line, often delaying the "suspense" of who or what is happening; for example, in Catullus 45, line 1 has *Acmen Septimus suos amores*, swinging down to line 2 for *tenens in gremio...*

HENDIADYS: a single idea expressed through two words, not usually taken together, which are joined by a conjunction, instead of a modified noun. For example, Ovid describes in *Amores* 1.9 his shaded couch as *lectus et umbra*.

HYPERBOLE: an exaggeration, purely for effect. The most obvious example from Catullus is the "How many of your kisses are enough...?" and the answer, among other exaggerations is *quam magnus numerus Libyssae harenae...*

IRONY: the implied meaning is actually the opposite of that which is stated. Horace illustrates this beautifully in *Ode* 1.23, where he has been urging his love in a SIMILE that she is not a fawn needing to fear fierce animals, but rather she is "ripe" for a man.

LITOTES: essentially a double negative; this figure affirms one thing by denying its opposite. Horace, in his *Ode* 1.23, compares a girl to a fawn who ventures out *non sine vano...*

METAPHOR: an implied comparison, without "like" or "as"; such as in Catullus 8: *fulsere quondam candidi tibi soles...*

METONYMY: a substitution of a word for another word or concept which it calls to mind. For example, in Catullus 45, *Venerem* (last line) represents love.

ONOMATOPOEIA: the use of a word whose sound suggests its meaning. Catullus, in Poem 3, "laments" the death of Lesbia's sparrow who used to *pipiabat* to its mistress alone.

OXYMORON: a contradiction in terms, as used by Horace in *Ode* 1.22 in his *arida nutrix*, a dry wet-nurse.

PERSONIFICATION: assigning human qualities or feelings to inanimate objects. Ovid animates the tablets in *Amores* 1.12, when he curses them, their words, and their wax, which brought him bad news.

PLEONASM: repetition for emphasis; or, using more words than are necessary to express an idea. Catullus, counting kisses with Lesbia, repeats *centum* and *mille* much more than is necessary to understand that they should kiss "a lot."

POLYSYNDETON: the use of more conjunctions than would be necessary just for meaning. Horace emphasizes his list of places by repeating *sive* and *vel* in *Ode* 1.22.

PROLEPSIS: mentioning a characteristic of something before it is logical, as in Ovid's *Amores* 1.9: leaders are seeking *animos in milite forti*

PROSOPOPOEIA: representing an imagined or absent person as speaking. Ovid approaches this as he puts words in Cupid's mouth in *Amores* 1.1: *Quodque canas, vates, accipe, dixit, opus.*

SIMILE: a comparison using "like" or "as"; Latin words are *similis, velut, qualis,* and *ut,* among others. Catullus 62, his *amoebean* hymn, compares a young woman to a flower in line 39: *ut flos...*

SYNCHYSIS: using interlocked word order, ABAB; as "noun adj. noun adj.," "nom. gen. nom. gen.," etc. See Horace, *Ode* 1.5, line 6–7: *...aspera nigris aequora ventis...*

SYNECDOCHE: a subset of METONYMY using a part for the whole from which it is made. For example *ferrea* referring to the iron weapons of war in Ovid's *Amores* 1.1.

TRANSFERRED EPITHET: using an adjective with one noun when it more properly applies to another; Catullus 51, line 11 illustrates this with *gemina teguntur lumina nocte.*

TRICOLON CRESCENS: a series of three words or phrases increasing in importance or intensity. One could find a proud Ovid as the third in a series in *Amores* 3.15: *Manuta Vergilio, gaudet Verona Catullo, Paelignae dicar gloria gentis ego...*

ZEUGMA: joining one word with two others, when logically it only goes with one of the words. In *Amores* 1.9, the lover *...ibit in adversos montes duplicataque nimbo flumine...* "...will go against opposing mountains and rivers doubled by rain." The verb must imply climbing in the first instance as well as swimming in the second.

SUGGESTED READINGS

CATULLUS

Arkins, R. "C. 7." *Analecta Classica* 48 (1979).

Bishop, J. D. "C. 70: A Poem and Its Hypothesis." *Helios* 15 (1988).

Commager, Steele. "The Structure of C. 5." *Classical Journal* 59 (1964).

Courtney, E. "Three Poems of Catullus: (1) Poem 62 and Its Greek Background." *Bulletin of the Institue of Classical Studies* 32 (1985).

Fredricksmeyer, E. A. "Observations on C. 5." *American Journal of Philology* 91 (1970).

Detmer, H. "C. 2B from a Structural Perspective." *Classical World* 78 (1984).

Genovese, E. N. "Symbolism in the Passer Poems" *Maia* 16 (1974).

Goud, T. "Who Speaks the Final Lines? C. 62: Structure and Ritual." *Phoenix* 49 (1993).

Greene, E. "Re-Figuring the Feminine Voice: Catullus Translating Sappho." *Arethusa* 32.1 (1996).

McCormick, P. J. "Reading and Interpreting C. 8." *Contemporary Literary Hermeneutics and Interpretation of Classical Texts*. Ottawa, 1981.

Miller, P. A. "Sappho 31 and C. 51: The Dialogism of Lyric." *Arethusa* 21 (1993).

Ross, D. O. "Style and Content in C. 45." *Classical Philology* 60 (1965).

Schmiel, R. "The Structure of C. 8: A History of Interpretation." *Classical Journal* 86 (1990–91).

Segal, C. "More Alexandrianism in C. VIII?" *Mnemosyne* 27 (1974).

Small, Stuart G. P. *Catullus, A Reader's Guide to the Poems*. University Press of America, 1983.

Thomas, R. F. "Sparrows, Hares, and Doves: A Catullan Metaphor and Its Tradition." *Helios* 20 (1993).

Thompson, D. F. S. *Catullus: Edited with a Textual and Interpretative Commentary.* University of Toronto Press, 1997.

Treggiari, S. *Roman Marriage: Justi Conjuges from the Time of Cicero to the Time of Ulpian.* Oxford University Press, 1993.

Vine, B. "On the Missing Fourth Stanza of C. 51." *Harvard Studies in Classical Philology* 94 (1992).

Wills, G. "Sappho 31 and Catullus 51." *Greek, Roman, and Byzantine Studies* 8 (1967).

Wiseman, T. P. *Catullus and his World.* Cambridge, 1985.

HORACE

Ancona, R. *Time and the Erotic in Horace's Odes.* Duke University Press, 1994.

Anderson, W. S. "Horace's Different Recommenders of *Carpe Diem* in C. 1.4, 7, 9, 11." *Classical Journal* 88 (1984).

Anderson, W. S., ed. *Why Horace? A Collection of Interpretations.* Bolchazy-Carducci Publishers, 1999.

Commager, Steele. *The Odes of Horace.* New Haven, 1962.

Fraenkel, E. *Horace.* Oxford University Press, 1957.

Garrison, D. H. *Horace: Epodes and Odes.* University of Oklahoma Press, 1991.

Helzle, M. "Eironeia in Horace's Odes 1.5 and 3.26." *Antichthon* 28 (1994).

Nielsen, R. "Horace's Odes 1.23: Innocence." *Arion* 9 (1970).

Nisbet, R., and M. Hubbard, "Commentary on Horace." *Odes I; II* (2 vol.), Oxford University Press, 1978.

Santirocco, M. *Unity and Design in Horace's Odes.* University of North Carolina Press, 1986.

Sutherland, E. H. "Audience Manipulation and Emotional Experience in Horace's 'Pyrra Ode'." *American Journal of Classical Philology* 116.3 (1995).

West, David. *Horace: Odes I, Carpe Diem:* Text, Translation, Commentary. Oxford, 1995.

Ovid

Barsby, J. *Ovid: Amores I.* Focus Publishing, 1979.

Boyd, Barbara Weiden. *Ovid's Literary Loves: Influence and Innovation in the Amores.* University of Michigan Press, 1997.

Davis, J. T. "Dramatic Pairings in the elegies of Propertius and Ovid." *Noctes Romanae* 15: Bern-Stuttgart, 1977.

Jestin, Charbra Adams, and Phyllis B. Katz. *Amores, Metamorphoses: Selections.* Bolchazy-Carducci Publishers, 1999.

Keith, Alison M. "Amores 1.1: Propertius and the Ovidian Programme." *Studies in Latin Literature and Roman History.* Carl Droux, ed. Coll. Latomus: Bruxelles, 1992.

McKeown, J. C. ed. "Ovid, Amores: Text, Prolegomena, and Commentary I, II, and III." *Arca, Classical and Medieval Texts, Papers and Monographs.* Leeds, 1987, 1989, 1998.

General Reading

Luck, Georg. *The Latin Love Elegy.* Robert Cunningham & Sons, Ltd. 1959.

Lyne, R. O. A. M. *The Latin Love Poets: from Catullus to Horace.* Clarendon Press. 1980.

The Augustan Age

Crawford, M. *The Roman Republic,* 2nd ed. Harvard University Press, 1992.

Galinsky, K. *Augustan Culture.* Princeton University Press, 1996.

Raaflaub, K. A., and M. Toher, eds., *Between Republic and Empire: Interpretation of Augustus and His Principate.* University of California Press, 1990.

Wells, C. *The Roman Empire.* 2nd ed. Harvard University Press, 1992.

BIBLIOGRAPHY

Ancona, Ronnie. *Horace: Selected Odes and Satire I.9.* Wauconda, IL: Bolchazy-Carducci Publishers, 1999.

Aronson, Andrew C., and Robert Boughner. *Catullus and Horace: Selections from their Lyric Poetry.* White Plains, NY: Longman, 1988.

Barnstone, Willis. *Sappho and the Greek Lyric Poets.* New York: Schocken Books, 1988.

Bennett, C. E. *Horace: Odes and Epodes.* Loeb Classical Library. Cambridge, MA: Harvard University Press, 1995.

Bennett, C. E. *Horace: Odes and Epodes.* College Classical Series. New Rochelle, NY: Caratzas Brothers Publishers, 1981.

Bowder, Diana. *Who Was Who in the Roman World.* New York: Washington Square Press, 1984.

Christ, Karl. *The Romans: An Introduction to Their History and Civilization.* Berkeley: California University Press, 1984.

Clancy, Joseph P. *The Odes and Epodes of Horace.* Chicago: The University of Chicago Press, 1960.

Cornish, F. W., J. P. Postgate, and J. W. Mackail, trans. *Catullus, Tibullus and Pervigilium Veneris.* Ed. G. P. Goold. Rev. 2nd ed. Loeb Classical Library. Cambridge, MA: Harvard University Press, 1962.

Fordyce, C. J. *Catullus: A Commentary.* Oxford: Oxford University Press, 1961.

Garrison, Daniel H. *The Student's Catullus.* 2nd ed. Oklahoma Ser. in Classical Culture. Norman: University of Oklahoma Press, 1995.

Gildersleeve, B. L., and G. Lodge. *Gildersleeve's Latin Grammar.* Wauconda, IL: Bolchazy-Carducci Publishers, 1997.

Goold, G. P. *Catullus.* Gerald Duckworth & Co. Ltd., 1983.

Grant, Michael. *The World of Rome.* New York: Meridian-Penguin Books, 1960.

Green, Ellen. "The Catullan Ego: Fragmentation and the Erotic Self." *American Journal of Philology* 116 (1995)

Greenough, J. B., G. L. Kittredge, A. A. Howard, and Benjamin L. D'Ooge, eds. *Allen and Greenough's New Latin Grammar*. New Rochelle: Aristide D. Caratzas Publisher, 1991.

Grimal, Pierre. *The Penguin Dictionary of Classical Mythology*. Stephen Kershaw, ed. New York: Penguin Books Ltd, 1990.

Gruen, Erich S. *The Last Generation of the Roman Republic*. Berkeley: University of California Press, 1974.

Hammond, Nicholas G. L. *Atlas of the Greek and Roman World in Antiquity*. New Jersey: Noyes Press, 1981.

Kenney, E. J. *P. Ovidi Nasonis: Amores, Medicamina Faciei Femineae, Ars Amatoria, Remedia Amoris*. Oxford: Oxford University Press, 1977.

LaFleur, Richard A. *Love and Transformation: An Ovid Reader*. Reading, MA: Addison-Wesley Publishing Co., 1995.

Lee, Guy, trans. *The Poems of Catullus*. Oxford World's Classics. Oxford: Oxford University Press, 1991.

LeGlay, Marcel, Jean-Louis Voisin, and Yann LeBohec. *A History of Rome*. Oxford: Blackwell Publishers, 1996.

Lewis, Charlton T. *An Elementary Latin Dictionary*. Oxford: Oxford University Press, 1891, 1993.

Lyne, R. O. A. M. *The Latin Love Poets From Catullus to Horace*. Oxford: Oxford University Press, 1980.

Martin, Charles. *Catullus*. New Haven: Yale University Press, 1992.

Martin, Charles, trans. *The Poems of Catullus*. Baltimore: Johns Hopkins University Press, 1990.

Morwood, James, ed. *The Oxford Latin Minidictionary*. Oxford: Oxford University Press, 1995.

Mynors, R. A. B. *C. Valerii Catulli: Carmina*. Oxford: Oxford University Press, 1958.

Radice, Betty. *Who's Who in the Ancient World*. Harmondsworth, UK: Penguin Books, Ltd., 1985.

Riddle, John M., J. WorthEstes, and Josiah C. Russell. "Ever Since Eve...Birth Control in the Ancient World." *Archaeology* Vol. 47, No. 2 (March/April, 1994).

Rose, H. J. *A Handbook of Greek Mythology*. New York: E. P. Dutton & Co., 1959.

Shepherd, W. G., trans. *Horace: The Complete Odes and Epodes with the Centennial Hymn.* London: Penguin Books, 1983.

Showerman, Grant, trans. *Ovid: Heroides and Amores.* 2nd Edition, revised by G. P. Goold. Cambridge: Harvard University Press, 1986.

Simpson, D. P., ed. *Cassell's Latin and English Dictionary.* New York: Macmillan Publishing Company, 1987.

Skinner, Marilyn B. "Ego Mulier: The Construction of Male Sexuality in Catullus." *Helios* 20 (1993).

Speake, Graham, ed. *Dictionary of Ancient History.* London: Penguin Books Ltd., 1994.

Watts, Niki. *The Oxford Paperback Greek Dictionary.* Oxford: Oxford University Press, 1997.

Wickham, Edward C., ed., and H. W. Garrod. *Q. Horati Flacci: Opera.* Oxford: Oxford Clarendon Press, 1941.

Zimmerman, J. E. *Dictionary of Classical Mythology.* New York: Bantam Books, Inc., 1971.

VOCABULARY

A

abdūcō, -dūcere, -dūxī, -ductus: take away, carry off

absūmō -sūmere, -sumpsī, -sumptus: consume, use up, waste

accipiō, -ere, -cēpī, -ceptus: receive, get, accept, take without effort

acer, -eris, n.: maple-wood, the maple tree

ācer, ācris, acre, adj.: sharp, piercing, penetrating

acquiēscō, -ere, -ēvi, —: become quiet, rest, repose

adeō, -īre, -iī, -itus: go to, come to, approach

adfectō / affectō, -āre, -āvī, -ātus: aim for, aspire to

adfluō, adfluere, adflūxī, adflūxus: flow freely, to flow on

adimō, adimere, adēmī, adēmptus: take away, deprive

adsum, adesse, adfuī, adfuturus (adfore): be present, be at hand

adulter, adultrī, m.: adulterer

adventus, -ūs, m.: a coming, an approach, arrival

adversus, -a, -um, adj.: turned towards, fronting, facing, before

adversus, adv.: opposite

advocō, -āre, -āvī, -ātus: call, summon, call to someone's aid

aedis, -is, f.: temple, sanctuary

aēneus, -a, -um, adj.: made of copper or bronze

aequālis, -e, adj.: equal, like, par

aequor, aequoris, n.: a flat, level surface, the sea

aequus, -a, -um, adj.: even, flat, fair

aes, aeris, n.: metal, copper, bronze; money, salary

aesculētum, -ī, n.: oak forest

aesculus, -ī, m.: oak tree

aestimō, -āre, -āvī, -ātus: value, rate, esteem

aestīvus, -a, -um, adj.: summer-like, summer

aestuōsus, -a, -um, adj.: hot, sweltering, burning

aetās, aetātis, f.: age, time, lifetime

agmen, agminis, n.: a driving movement; herd or flock (of animals); army on the march

āgnus, -ī, m.: lamb

agō, agere, ēgī, āctus: do, drive, compel

agricola, -ae, m.: farmer

Albanus, -a, -um, adj.: alban, pertaining to the Alban hills in Italy

āles, āletis, adj.: winged

alius, alia, aliud, pronoun: another, other, different

alumnus, -ī, m.: nursling, foster-son

amābilis, -e, adj.: lovely, lovable, amicable

ambitiōsus, -a, -um, adj.: ambitious, eager for honor; surrounding, encompassing

ambo, ambae, ambō, adj.: both

ambūrō, amburere, ambūssī, ambūstus: burn

āmittō, -ere, -īsī, -īssus: send away, dismiss, part with

amo, -āre, -āvī, -ātus: love, regard

amor, amōris, m.: love, desire, fondness

Amor (amor), amōris, m.: Cupid, love, affection

ancilla, -ae, f.: servant

angiportus, -ūs, m.: narrow street, alley

anguis, -is, m. and f.: snake

animus, -ī, m.: soul, spirit, the seat of feeling or rational principle

annus, -ī, m.: year, circle of the sun

ante, prep. + acc.: before, in front of

antrum, -ī, n.: hollow (of a tree)

anus, -ūs, f.: old woman

apis, -is, f.: a bee

apium, -ī, n.: parsley

appetēns, -entis, adj.: eager for, desirous of

approbātiō, -ōnis, *f.:* an approval, approbation

aqua, -ae, *f.:* water

aquōsus, -a, -um, *adj.:* watery, rain-bearing

āra, -ae, *f.:* altar, either in a temple or the home

arātrum, -ī, *n.:* a plough

arbitrium, -ī, *n.:* a judgment, decision

arcus, -ūs, *m.:* a bow

ārdēns, -entis, *adj.:* glowing, fiery, hot, ablaze

ārdeō, -ēre, arsī, arsus: be on fire, burn, blaze

ardor, -ōris, *m.:* flame, a burning

arduus, -a, -um, *adj.:* steep, lofty, high

argentum, -ī, *n.:* silver

āridus, -a, -um, *adj.:* dry, barren, weathered

arma, -ōrum *(pl.), n.:* arms, weaponry, tools, *(fig.* phallus)

arrogāns, arrogantis, *adj.:* arrogant

artūs, -uum *(pl. only), m.:* limbs, joints

arvus, -a, -um, *adj.:* ploughed *(as subs.:* ploughed field)

ās, assis, *m.:* a copper unit, the unit of money

asper, aspera, asperum, *adj.:* fierce, rough

asperō, -āre, -āvī, -ātus: make fierce, violent, harsh

aspiciō, -ere, -ēxī, -ectus: look at, behold, look upon

assidue (adsidue), *adv.:* continually, constantly

at, *conjunction:* but

āter, -tra, -trum, *adj.:* black, dark, gloomy, sad

atquī, *conjunction:* nevertheless

attenuō, -āre, -āvī, -ātus: reduce, weaken, lessen, diminish

auctor, auctōris, *m.:* an originator, creator, founder, author

audiō, audīre, audīvī, audītus: hear

aura, -ae, *f.:* breeze, air, breath of air

aureolus, -a, -um, *diminutive:* golden

aureus, -a, -um, *adj.:* golden

auris, -is, *f.:* ear

auspicātus, -a, -um, *adj.:* consecrated, favorable, fortunate

auspicor, -ārī, -ātus sum, *deponent verb:* take the auspices

avārus, -a, -um, *adj.:* greedy, desirous, grasping

āvellō, -ere, -vellī, volsus (vulsus): tear away, pluck, snatch, seize

aveō, avēre, avui, avutus: wish, desire

āversus, -a, -um, *adj.:* turned from, disinclined

avidus, -a, -um, *adj.:* eager, desirous

āvius, -a, -um, *adj.:* pathless, no road or pathway

B

bacchor, bacchārī, bacchātus sum, *deponent verb:* celebrate the feast of Bacchus, revel, run wild, riot *(generally used with orgiastic overtones)*

barbarus, -a, -um, *adj.:* barbarian, foreign, cruel

barbitos, barbitos *(Greek nom.),* **barbite** *(voc.),* **barbiton** *(Greek acc.): m. and f.:* the lyre *(a stringed musical instrument)*

bāsiātiō, -ōnis, *f.:* a kissing, kiss

bāsiō, -āre, -āvī, -ātus: kiss

bāsium, -ī, *n.:* a kiss

beātus, -a, -um, *adj.:* fortunate, blessed, prosperous

bellum, -ī, *n.:* war

bibō, bibere, bibī, —: drink, absorb, imbibe

bis, *adv.:* twice, in two ways

bracchium, -ī, *n.:* arm

brevis, -e, *adj.:* short, small, shallow, brief

būbō, -ōnis, *m.:* horned owl

C

cadō, cadere, cecidī, casūrus: fall, be slain

cadus, -ī, *m.:* large jar for storing wine

caelestis, -e, *adj.:* belonging to heaven, divine, heavenly

caelum, -ī, *n.:* sky, heaven, vault of heaven

caesius, -a, -um, *adj.:* of a blue-grey color *(of the eyes only)*

caleō, -ēre, -uī, —: be in love with

campus, -ī, *m.:* field, plain

candidus, -a, -um, *adj.:* glittering, white, shiny white, clear, bright

canis, -is, *m. and f.:* dog

canō, -ere, cecinī, —: sing, sound

cantō, -āre, -āvī, -ātus: sing

cānus, -a, -um, *adj.*: white, hoary, whitened

captīvus, -a, -um, *adj.*: captured, captive

caput, -itis, *n.*: head

cardō, cardinis, *m.*: hinge

careo, -ēre, -uī, -itūrus (+ *abl.*): be without, be free from

cariōsus, -a, -um, *adj.*: dried up, decayed

carmen, carminis, *n.*: song, poem

carnifex, -icis, *m.*: executioner, hangman

carpō, -ere, -psī, -ptus: pick, pluck, pluck off, enjoy, use, consume

cārus, -a, -um, *adj.*: dear

castus, -a, -um, *adj.*: pure, holy, sacred

caterva, -ae, *f.*: crowd, throng

causor, -ārī, -ātus sum, *deponent verb:* use as an excuse, plead, pretend

cautus, -a, -um, *adj.*: cautious, wary, provident

cēra, -ae, *f.*: wax

Cerēs, Cereris, *f.*: Ceres (*Goddess of agriculture, daughter of Saturn*)

certē, *adv.*: certainly

certest (= certum est): it is certain

cervix (cervēx), cervīcis: *f.*: the neck

cessō, -āre, -āvī, -ātus: delay, be remiss, loiter, cease

cēterus, -a, -um, *adj.*: the other, remainder, rest

cicūta, -ae, *f.*: hemlock (*used as a poison*)

cithara, -ae, *f.*: a stringed instrument, lyre

clārus, -a, -um, *adj.*: clear, bright, brilliant, distinguished, famous

claudō, claudere, clausī, clausus: close, conclude

cōgnitor, -ōris, *m.*: advocate, attorney

cōgō, -ere, coēgī, coāctus: drive together, collect, crowd, bring together, summon

colligō, -ere, -lēgī, -lectus: gather, collect

collum, -ī, *n.*: neck

colō, -ere, coluī, cultus: look after, tend to, till

color, colōris, *m.*: color, complexion

coma, -ae, *f.*: hair

commendō, -āre, -āvī, -ātus: entrust, confide, deposit with

committō, -mittere, -mīsī, -missus: unite, combine, entrust

comō, comere, compsī, comptus: put together, make neat, arrange, comb

compēs, compedis, *f.*: shackle, foot iron

complexus, -ūs, *m.*: a surrounding, encompassing, embrace, clasp

comprimō, -ere, -pressī, -pressus: compress, squeeze tightly

condiscō, -discere, -didicī, —: learn thoroughly

cōnfiteor, -ērī, -fessus sum, *deponent verb:* acknowledge, confess, own, avow

congerō, -ere, -gessī, -gestus: collect, heap up

cōnsurgō, -ere, -surrēxī, -surrēctus: rise, stand up, arise, rise in a body

contingō, -ere, -tigī, -tāctus: touch, reach, take hold of, seize

continuō, *adv.*: straightaway, immediately

conturbō, -āre, -āvī, -ātus: confuse, disturb, disorder, confound

cōnūbium, -ī, *n.*: marriage, wedlock

convellō, -ere, -vellī, -volsus (vulsus): tear away, pull off, pluck up

conveniō, -īre, -vēnī, -ventus: agree, come together on, be fit or suitable

convertō, -ere, -tī, -sus: turn around, cause to turn, turn back

convincō, -vincere, -vīcī, -victus: convict, prove wrong

cor, cordis, *n.*: heart

corniger, -gera, -gerum, *adj.*: horned, horn-bearing

corōna, -ae, *f.*: crown, garland

corpus, -oris, *n.*: body

cortex, corticis, *m. and f.*: bark, cork, shell

corvus, -ī, *m.*: a raven, grappling-iron

crēber, -bra, -brum, *adj.*: repeated, frequent, numerous

crēdibilis, -e, *adj.*: believable, credible

crēdō, -ere, -didī, -ditus: lend, entrust, believe, have confidence in, trust

crēdulus, -a, -um, *adj.*: trusting, believing easily

crīnis, -is, *m.*: hair

crūdēlis, -e, *adj.*: rude, unfeeling, hard, cruel, severe

cūnctus, -a, -um, *adj.*: all, together, joint

cūra, -ae, *f.*: care, trouble, attention

cūriōsus, -a, -um, *adj.*: careful, diligent, attentive, curious

currō, currere, cucurrī, cursus: run, hurry

currus, -ūs, *m.:* chariot

cursō, -āre, —, —: run here and there

curvō, -āre, -āvī, -ātus: bend, arch, curve

cuspis, cuspidis, *f.:* point, spear

custōdia, -ae, *f.:* a watching, watch, guard, care, protection

Cryene, -es *and* **Cyrenae, -arum,** *f.:* a city of N.E. Africa (*birthplace of the poet Callimachus*)

Cytherea, -ae, *f.:* Venus

D

dē, *prep. + abl.:* from, concerning, by reason of

dēbilitō, -āre, -āvī, -ātus: weaken, break down, debilitate

decet, -ēre, -uit, —: become, behoove, fitting (**decet,** it is fitting)

decorō, -āre, -āvī, -ātus: adorn, glorify, grace

dēdeceō, -ēre, -cuī, —: disgrace, disfigure

dēdicō, -āre, -āvī, -ātus: dedicate

dēdūcō, ducere, dūxī, ductus: draw apart, separate

dēflōrēscō, deflorescere, deflorui, —: deflower, fade, wither (*fig.* lose one's virginity)

dēfungor, fungī, fūnctus sum, *deponent verb:* finish, discharge

deinde (dein), *adv.:* then, thereafter, next

dēliciae, -ārum (*pl. only*), *f.:* a delight, pleasure, charm, voluptuousness

dēligō, deligere, delēgi, delēctus: pick, choose, or select

dēmānō, -āre, —, —: flow down, glide down

dēprēndō, -ere, -dī, -sus: take away, seize upon, catch

dēserō, dēserere, dēseruī, dēsertus: abandon, desert

dēserviō, -īre, —, —: serve zealously

dēsīderium, -ī, *n.:* a longing, ardent desire, wish, want

dēsidia, -ae, *f.:* laziness, leisure

dēsidiōsus, -a, -um, *adj.:* slothful, indolent, lazy

dēsinō, -ere, dēstitī (desiī), -situs: cease, desist, give over

dēspondeō, -ēre, spondī, spōnsus: promise to give, promise, pledge

dēsultor, -ōris, *m.:* a vaulter, circus-rider, inconstant one

diēs, -ēī, *m.:* day, daylight

difficilis, -e, *adj.:* difficult, hard to deal with

digitus, -ī, *m.:* a finger, toe

dīgnus, -a, -um, *adj.:* worthy, deserving of, suitable, fitting, proper

dīligō, -ere, -lēxī, -lēctus: single out, esteem, value

dīmoveō, -ēre, -ōvī, -ōtus: move apart

dispār, disparis, *adj.:* unequal, unlike

dispereō, -īre, -iī, —: go to ruin, be undone, it's all over with me

dīstinctus, -a, -um, *adj.:* distinct, separate, eminent

diū, *adv.:* a long time, long while

dīva, -ae, *f.:* goddess

dīves, -itis, *adj.:* rich, wealthy

dīvidō, -ere, -vīsī, -vīsus: divide, part

dō, dare, dedī, datus: give, hand over, deliver

doceō, docēre, docuī, doctus: teach, instruct, inform

doleō, -ēre, -uī, -itūrus: suffer, feel pain, be in pain, ache

dolor, -ōris, *m.:* a pain, suffering, anguish

dominus, -ī, *m.:* master, possessor, ruler, lord, owner

domus, -ūs, *f.:* house, home

dōnec, *adv.:* as long as

dormiō, -īre, -īvī, -ītus: rest, sleep, be inactive

dōs, -ōtis, *f.:* dowry, marriage portion

dubitō, -āre, -āvī, -ātus: be in doubt, waver, be uncertain

dūcō, -ere, -ūxī, -uctus: lead, conduct, guide, direct

dulcis, -e, *adj.:* sweet, dear, endearing, charming

dulciter, *adv.:* sweetly

duplex, -icis, *adj.:* double, two-faced

duplicātus, -a, -um, *adj.:* doubled

duplicō, -āre, -āvī, -ātus: double, multiply by two, repeat

E

ēbrius, -a, -um, *adj.:* drunk, intoxicated, full, sated

ēdō, edere, edidī, editus: put forth, publish

ēducō, -āre, -āvī, -ātus: bring up, rear, train, educate

ēdūcō, -ere, -dūxī, -ductus: lead forth, draw out, bring off

effodiō, -ere, -fōdī, -fossus: dig out, mine, excavate, dig up

effūsus, -a, -um, *adj.:* poured out, extensive, vast

ēmīror, emīrārī, —, *deponent verb:* wonder at

ēmodulor, -arī, —, *deponent verb:* sing, celebrate

ephēmeris, -idis, *f.:* day-book, diary

eques, equitis, *m.:* horseman, knight, one who rides a horse

equidem, *adv.:* truly, verily, indeed, at all events

ēripiō, -ere, -ipuī, -eptus: tear out, snatch away, grab, pluck

excutiō, excutere, excussī, excussus: shake out, throw out, shake off

exemplum, -ī, *n.:* a sample, example, precedent, warning, object-lesson

eximō, -ere, -ēmī, -ēmptus: take away, remove

exitium, -iī, *n.:* mischief, ruin, death

expediō, expedīre, expedīvī, expedītus: dismiss, free, release

experiēns, experientis, (from *experior*) enterprising

exsecō, -āre, -cuī, -ctus: cut out, cut away, remove

exsolvō, -ere, -solvī, -solūtus: loose, unloose, set loose, release, deliver

exspectō, -āre, -āvī, -ātus: look out for, await, wait for,

exsultō, -āre, -āvī, —: spring vigorously, leap up, jump up

exterō, -ere, —, —: crush, tread upon

exterreō, -ēre, -uī, -itus: frighten, scare

extollō, -ere, —, —: lift out, lift up, raise

extrēmum, -ī, *n.:* limit, outside, far away place

F

fabrīlis, -e, *adj.:* of the craftsman (*especially Vulcan*)

fābulōsus, -a, -um, *adj.:* fabled, legendary

facilis, -e, *adj.:* easy, without difficulty, easy to do

faciō, facere, fēcī, factus: make, do, construct, fashion

fallāx, fallācis, *adj.:* deceitful, false

fascinō, -āre, —, —: enchant, fascinate

fātum, -ī, *n.:* oracle, prophetic declaration

fax, facis, *f.:* torch (*especially a wedding torch*)

fēlīx, -īcis, *adj.:* productive, fruitful

fenestra, -ae, *f.:* window

ferō, ferre, tulī, lātus: carry, bring, plunder; **fertur,** it is said

ferreus, -a, -um, *adj.:* iron, hard, cruel, firm

fessus, -a, -um, *adj.:* tired

festīnō, -āre, -āvī, -ātus: hurry, rush about

fīctūm, -ī, *n.:* a deception, falsehood

fīctus, -a, -um, *adj.:* feigned, false, fictitious

fidēlis, -e, *adj.:* faithful, trusty

fidēs, -ei or **-ē, fidē** (*rare gen.*), *f.:* trust, faith, confidence

fīlum, -ī, *n.:* thread, string

findō, findere, -fidī, fissus: divide, split into two parts

fīnis, -is, *m.:* boundary, limit, border; aim

fīrmō, -āre, -āvī, -ātus: make firm, strengthen, fortify

fīrmus, -a, -um, *adj.:* firm, strong, stable, steadfast

flagellum, -ī, *n., diminutive:* a whip, scourge, a lash, sting

flagrāns, flagrantis, *adj.:* blazing, passionate

flamma, -ae, *f.:* blaze, fire, flame

flāvēns, -ntis, *adj.:* light yellow, golden yellow

flāvus, -a, -um, *adj.:* blonde, golden yellow

fleō, flēre, flēvī, flētus: mourn, weep (for)

flōs, -ōris, *m.:* a blossom, flower

flūmineus, -a, -um, *adj.:* of a river (*e.g. river-water*)

foedus, -eris, *n.:* treaty, pact, alliance, agreement

folium, -ī, *n.:* leaf

fōrma, -ae, *f.:* form, figure, beauty

forēs (foris), -um *(pl. only),* *f.:* door, gate, entrance

fōrmōsus, -a, -um, *adj.:* beautiful, striking, finely formed

fōrtasse, *adv.:* perhaps, it may be that

frangō, -ere, frēgi, frāctus: shatter, fracture, break into pieces, weaken, break

fretum, -ī, *n.:* straits, channel, sea

frōns, frōndis, *f.:* leaf

fruor, fruī, frūctus sum *(+ abl.), deponent verb:* enjoy, delight in

frūstrā, *adv.:* in deception, in error

fugiō, -ere, fūgī, fugitus: flee, fly, take flight, pass away

fulgeō, -ēre, fulsī, —: flash, glitter, gleam, glare

fulgor, fulgōris, *m.:* glitter, shine

fūmus, -ī, *m.:* smoke, vapor, steam

fūnāle, -is, *n.:* wax-torch

fūnebria, -e, *adj.:* of a funeral

fūnis, -is, *m.:* rope, cable

fūr, fūris, *m.:* thief, rogue

furiō, -āre, -āvī, -ātus: enrage, madden, make furious

fūrtīvus, -a, -um, *adj.:* stolen, purloined, pilfered

G

galea, -ae, *f.:* helmet, head-piece

ganniō, -īre, —, —: bark, snarl, growl

garrulus, -a, -um, *adj.:* chattering, prattling, talkative

gaudeō, -ēre, gāvīsus sum *(+ abl.), semideponent verb:* rejoice, delight in

gaudium, -ī, *n.:* joy, happiness

geminus, -a, -um, *adj.:* born together, twin

gener, -ī, *m.:* son-in-law

generō, -āre, -āvī, -ātus: produce, beget

geniālis, -is, -e, *adj.:* genial, merry

genū, -ūs, *n.:* knee

genus, generis, *n.:* birth, origin, race, family

gesta, -ōrum, *n.:* deeds, acts, achievements

glaciō, -āre, -āvī, -ātus: freeze

gnātus, -a, -um: born, made, destined

gracilis, -e, *adj.:* slender

graphium, -ī, *n.:* pen, stylus

grātus, -a, -um, *adj.:* pleasing, agreeable, deserving, thanks

gravātus, -a, -um, *adj.:* weighed down

gravidus, -a, -um *(+ abl.), adj.:* heavy, filled with

gravis, -e, *adj.:* heavy, weighty, important, serious, burdened

gremium, -ī, *n.:* lap, bosom

guttur, -uris, *n.:* the gullet, throat, neck

H

habeō, -ēre, -uī, -itus: have, hold, support, carry, regard

habilis, -e, *adj.:* fit, apt, suitable

harēna, -ae, *f.:* sand

hedera, -ae, *f.:* ivy

heu, *interjection:* alas

hiems, hiemis, *f.:* winter, storm

homō, -inis, *m. and f.:* a human being, man, person

hōra, -ae, *f.:* an hour, time of day

hortor, -ārī, -ātus, *deponent verb:* urge, press, incite

hortus, -ī, *m.:* a garden, park

hostis, -is, *m. and f.:* stranger, enemy, foreigner

I

iaceō, -ēre, -cuī, —: lie, be prostrate

iactus, -ūs, *m.:* throwing, cast

iaculum, -ī, *n.:* dart, javelin

iānua, -ae, *f.:* door, entrance

īcō *or* **icio, -ere, -īcī, -ictus:** strike, smite, stab

identidem, *adv.:* again, often, repeatedly

idōneus, -a, -um, *adj.:* fit, suitable, appropriate

Idūs, -uum, *f. (pl.):* the Ides (*the middle of the month in the Roman calendar*)

iecur, iecoris, *n.:* liver

īgnis, -is, *m.:* fire

īgnōtus, -a, -um, *adj.:* unknown, strange, unfamiliar

imber, imbris, *m.:* rain, heavy rain, shower

immolo, -āre, -āvī, -ātus: offer a sacrifice

immundus, -a, -um, *adj.:* unclean, impure

impēnsē, *adv.:* greatly, exceedingly, very much

impotēns, -entis, *adj.:* powerless, weak, impotent

improbus, -a, -um, *adj.:* inferior, bad, perverse, not up to par

imputō, -āre, -āvī, -ātus: reckon, attribute, make account of

inbellis, -e, *adj.:* not warlike, peaceful

incipiō, -ere, -cēpī, -ceptus: take hold, take in hand; begin

incitō, -āre, -āvī, -ātus: set in rapid motion, urge on, hasten, quicken

incola, -ae, *m. and f.:* inhabitant, resident

increpō, -āre, -uī, -itus: make a loud noise, protest at

indicō, -āre, -āvī, -ātus: proclaim, show

ineptiō, -īre, —, —: be absurd, trifle, play the fool

inermis, -e, *adj.:* unarmed, helpless, defenseless

ingenium, -ī, *n.:* temperament, character, general nature, intelligence

ingrātus, -a, -um, *adj.:* unpleasant, ungrateful

inhorrēscō, inhorrescere, inhorruī, —, *inceptive verb:* begin to tremble, shiver

inhospitālis, -e, *adj.:* inhospitable, unwelcoming

inimīcus, -a, -um, *adj.:* hostile, unfriendly, inimical

inīquus, -a, -um, *adj.:* unkind, hostile

innūptus, -a, -um, *adj.:* unmarried, unwedded, single

inquīrō, -ere, -sīvī, -sītus: seek after, search for, look into

īnsolēns, -ntis, *adj.:* surprised, inexperienced

īnstruō, -struere, -struxī, -structus: set up, build, prepare, furnish with

intāctus, -a, -um, *adj.:* untouched, uninjured, intact

integer, integra, integrum, *adj.:* complete, whole, pure, innocent, sound

intemptātus, -a, -um, *adj.:* untried

inter, *prep. + acc.:* between, among

intereō, -īre, -iī, -itūrus: go among, be lost

interlūnium, interluniī, *n.:* the time/the dark moon that is before the new moon

intestīnum, -ī, *n.:* a gut, intestines, entrails

inuleus (hinnuleus), -ī, *m.:* young stag, fawn

inūtilis, -e, *adj.:* useless, worthless

invicem, *adv.:* in turn, alternately

invideō, -ēre, -vīdī, -vīsus: cast an evil eye upon

invidia, -ae, *f.:* envy, jealousy

invidus, -a, -um, *adj.:* envious, grudging

invīsō, -ere, -sī: look after, go to see

invītus, -a, -um, *adj.:* against the will, unwilling, reluctant

iocor, -ārī, -ātus sum: jest, joke

iocōsus, -a, -um, *adj.:* full of jesting, humorous, droll

īrācundus, -a, -um, *adj.:* inclined to anger or rage, irascible, passionate

īrātus, -a, -um, *adj.:* angered, angry, enraged

iter, itineris, *n.:* journey

iūcundus, -a, -um, *adj.:* pleasant, agreeable

iugōsus, -a, -um, *adj.:* mountainous

iugum, -ī, *n.:* yoke, collar on an oxen team (*joining them together*)

iungō, iungere, iūnxī, iūnctus: join together, unite, connect

iūre, *adv.:* rightly, deservedly

iūs, iūris, *n.:* that which is just, right

iuvencus, -ī, *m.:* a young bull

iuvenis, -is, *adj.:* young, youthful

L

labellum, -ī, *n., diminutive:* a small lip

labōrō, -āre, -āvī, -ātus: labor, take pains, trouble

lacerta, -ae, *f.:* lizard

laetitia, -ae, *f.:* joy, exultation, rejoicing

laevus, -a, -um, *adj.:* left, left side

lambō, lambere, lambi: lick, lap, splash

lāsarpīcifer, -fera, -ferum, *adj.:* producing asafoetida

lascīvus, -a, -um: playful, wanton, lustful, insolent

lassō, -āre, -āvī, -ātus: tire, make weary

lateō, -ēre, -uī, —: lurk, lie hidden, be concealed

latus, latēris, *n.:* side, flank, *(implying body)*

lātus, -a, -um: wide, broad

laudō, -āre, -āvī, -ātus: praise

leō, leonis, *m.:* lion

levis, -e: light

leviter, *adv.:* lightly

levō, -āre, -āvī, -ātus: lift up, raise up, lighten, relieve

libēns, libentis, *adj.:* willing, with pleasure, willingly

libīdō, libīdinis, *f.:* pleasure, desire, eagerness, lust

licet, -ēre, -cuit, —, *impersonal verb:* it is permitted, it is allowed

ligō, -āre, -āvī, -ātus: tie, bind, bind together

līmen, liminis, *n.:* threshold

lingua, -ae, *f.:* tongue, language, speech

linquō, -ere, līquī, —: leave, quit, depart from; forsake

liquidus, -a, -um: fluid, flowing

liquō, -āre, -āvī, -ātus: strain, decant *(the wine before serving to remove sediment)*

loquor, loquī, locūtus sum, *deponent verb:* speak, say, talk

lubet (libet), -ēre, libuit, —, *impersonal verb:* it pleases, is pleasing

lūcidus, -a, -um, *adj.:* clear, bright, full of light

lucrum, -ī, *n.:* greed, profit, gain

lūdō, -ere, -sī, -sus: play, play at a game

lumen, -inis, *n.:* light, lamp-light

lūnō, -āre, -āvī, -ātus: bend like a half-moon

lupus, -ī, *m.:* a wolf

lūstrum, -ī, *n.:* a five-year period of time

lūx, lūcis, *f.:* light, brightness, daylight, elucidation

Lydia, -ae, *f.:* Lydia *(a country in Asia Minor; a woman's name)*

M

maereō, maerēre, —, —, *intransitive verb:* grieve, mourn

mālō (māvolō), mālle, māluī, —: choose rather, prefer

mālum, -ī, *n.:* an apple

malus, -a, -um, *adj.:* bad, not good, mean

mandō, -āre, -āvī, -ātus: give over, entrust

māne, n., adv.: early in the morning

maneō, -ēre, mānsī, mānsus: stay, remain, abide

manus, -ūs, *f.:* hand, *(in the pl.,* band, group)

mare, maris, *n.:* the sea

margō, -inis, *m. and f.:* edge, border, margin

marīnus, -a, -um: of the sea

marītus, -a, -um, *adj.:* nuptual, of marriage; *(as subst.,* a married man, husband)

māteria, -ae, *f.:* subject matter, material

mātūrus, -a, -um, *adj.:* ripe, mature, of age

Maurus, -a, -um, *adj.:* Moorish, African

meditor, -ārī, -ātus, *deponent verb:* reflect, muse, consider, give attention to

medulla, -ae, *f.:* marrow, heart, innermost part

mel, mellis, *n.:* honey

melior, melius *(comp. adj. from* **bonus**): better

membrum, -ī, *n.:* a limb, member, *(in the pl.,* the body)

meminī, -isse *(only in perf.):* recollect, remember, think of

memorābilis, -e, *adj.:* heard of, credible, that may be told of

mēns, mentis, *f.:* the mind, disposition, feeling, character

mēnsa, -ae, *f.:* table

mēnsis, -is, *m.:* month

mereō, -ēre, -uī, -itus: deserve, earn

mēta, -ae, *f.:* goal, turning-post

metuō, metuere, metuī, —: fear, be afraid

metus, -ūs, *m.:* fear

mica, -ae, *f.:* a crumb, bit, morsel

mīles, -itis, *m.:* soldier

mīlitāris, -e, *adj.:* military, warlike

mīlitia, -ae, *f.:* military service, warfare

mīlitō, -āre, -āvī, -ātus: serve in the military, be a soldier

mināx, minacis, *f., as a noun and adj.:* projecting, overhanging, threatening, menacing

minium, -ī, *n.:* cinnabar *(a red dye and medicinal agent)*

minuō, minuere, minuī, minūtus: make smaller, diminish, lessen

mīrus, -a, -um, *adj.:* wonderful, marvelous, amazing

misellus, -a, -um, *diminutive adj.:* poor, wretched, unfortunate miser, -era, -erum, *adj.:* wretched, unfortunate, miserable

mītis, -e, *adj.:* soft, mild

mōbilis, -e, *adj.:* stirring, mobile, changeable

modus, -ī, *m.:* measure, rhythm, limit, rule, manner, mode, way

modus, -ī, *m.:* measure, size, rhythm

moechus, -ī, *m.:* adulterer

molestus, -a, -um, *adj.:* troublesome, irksome, grievous

molliō, -īre, -īvī, -ītus: soften, weaken

mollis, -e, *adj.:* flexible, pliant, yielding, supple, gentle

mōns, mōntis, *m.:* mountain

mordeō, -ēre, momordī, morsus: bite, bite into; take hold of

morior, morī (morīrī), mortuus sum: die

morsus, -ūs, *m.:* a biting, bite, sting, pain, vexation

mōs, mōris, *m.:* a will, way, habit, manner

moveō, movēre, mōvī, mōtus: move

mulceō, -ēre, -sī, -sus: stroke, graze, touch lightly, fondle

mulier, -eris, *f.:* woman, female

munditia, -ae, *f.:* elegance, neatness, cleanliness

mūnus, mūneris, *n.:* a public office, an affectionate service, rites for the dead

mūtuus, -a, -um, *adj.:* mutual, interchangeable, reciprocal

myrtus, -ī, *f.:* myrtle

N

nam, *conjunction:* for

nāscor, -ī, nātus sum, *deponent verb:* be born, begin life, be produced

nātālis, -is, *n.:* birthday

nātus, -a, -um, *adj.:* child of, born of

nātus, -ī, *m.:* son of

nātus, -a, -um, *adj.:* born, made, destined, designed

nebula, -ae, *f.:* cloud

nectō, nectere, nexuī (nexī), nexus: tie, bend, fasten, bind up

nefās, *n., indeclinable noun:* crime, sin, abomination

negō, -āre, -āvī, -ātus: refuse, refute, negate, decline, deny

nempe, *conjunction:* certainly, without doubt

nemus, nemoris, *n.:* grove, woods

nervus, -ī, *m.:* tendon, sinew, string (of musical instrument), strap

nēsciō, -īre, -īvī, -itus: not to know, be ignorant; nescio quid + *gen.*, some sort of...

nēscius, -a, -um: not known, unaware

nimbus, -ī, *m.:* rain-storm, cloud

nīmīrum, *adv.:* without doubt, surely, truly

nimium, *adv.:* too much, too

niteō, nitēre, nituī, —: shine, sparkle

nītor, -ī, nīxus sum, *deponent verb:* bear upon, press upon, lean, support oneself

nix, nivis, *f.:* snow

nōlō, nōlle, nōluī, —: not to wish, not wish, be unwilling

nōmen, -inis, *n.:* name, renown

nōscō, -ere, nōvī, nōtus: learn, come to know, discern, investigate, recognize

notātus, -a, -um, *adj.:* known, marked

nōtus, -a, -um, *adj.:* known, regarded

nox, noctis, *f.:* night

nūbō, -ere, nūpsī, nūptus: be married, marry, wed

nūdus, -a, -um, *adj.:* naked, stripped, unclothed

nūmen, nūminis, *n.:* divine will, divine presence, bias, nod; deity

numquam, *adv.:* never, at no time ever

nūper, *adv.:* recently, not long ago, lately

nūpta, -ae , *f.:* wife

nūtrīx, nūtrīcis, *f.:* nurse

O

obdūrō, -āre, -āvī, -ātus: be hard, hold out, persist, endure

obeō, obīre, obīvī, obitus: go to or towards, go against or oppose; die

obiciō, obicere, obiēcī, obiectus: throw before

oblīvīscor, -ī, -lītus sum, *deponent verb:* forget, neglect, omit

obloquor, -ī, -locūtus sum, *deponent verb:* speak against, interrupt, contradict

obsideō, -ēre, -ēdī, -essus: sit, abide, remain

obstinātus, -a, -um, *adj.:* resolved, determined, resolute, steadfast

obstipēscō, -ere, -puī, —: be astounded or stupefied

obvius, -a, -um, *adj.:* in the way, so as to meet, meeting, to meet

occidō, -ere, -cidī, -cāsus: fall down, fall, go down; set

occupō, -āre, -āvī, -ātus: take possession of, seize, embrace, occupy

ocellus, -ī, *m., diminutive:* a little eye

octāvus, -a, -um, *adj.:* eighth

ōdī, ōdisse, ōsūrus, *defective verb:* hate

odor, odoris, *m.:* fragrance, perfume

oppositus, -a, -um, *adj.:* opposite, standing against

ops, opis, *f.:* aid, help, strength

optātus, -a, -um, *adj.:* wished, desired, longed for

optō, -āre, -āvī, -ātus: choose, select, prefer

opus, -eris, *n.:* work, labor necessity; **opus est,** it is necessary

ōrāclum (= oraculum), -ī, *n.:* a divine announcement, an oracle

ōrdinō, -āre, -āvī, -ātus: set or arrange in order

ōs, ōris, *n.:* mouth

ostendō, -ere, -dī, -tus: stretch out, spread before, expose to view

ōtium, -ī, *n.:* leisure, vacant time, freedom from business

P

paelex (pellex), paelicis (pellicis), *f.:* mistress, a concubine of a married man

paene, *adv.:* almost

pallor, pallōris, *m.:* paleness *(especially from emotion)*

palma, -ae, *f.:* the palm, flat hand

pangō, -ere, pepigī (pēgī), pāctus: fasten, make fast, fix, drive in

pār, paris, *adj.:* equal

parcē, *adv.:* sparingly

parcō, parcere, pepercī (parsī), parsus: spare, refrain from injuring

parcus, -a, -um, *adj.:* frugal, thrifty

parēns, -entis, *m. and f.:* a procreator, father, mother, parent

pāreō, -ēre, -uī, —: appear, be visible, be at hand

pariēs, pariētis, *m.:* a wall, especially a wall in a house

parō, -āre, -āvī, -ātus: make ready, prepare, furnish, provide

pars, partis, *f.:* a part, piece, portion, share

passer, -eris, *m.:* sparrow

patior, -ī, passus sum, *deponent verb:* suffer, bear, endure, allow

pavidus, -a, -um, *adj.:* frightened, trembling

pellō, -ere, pepulī, pulsus: strike, break, hit, impel, propel

Penātēs, Penātium *(pl.), m.:* household gods

penitus, *adv.:* inwardly, deeply, far within

perarō, -āre, -āvī, -ātus: plough through, write, inscribe

perditē, *adv.:* recklessly, desperately

perdō, -ere, -didī, -ditus: make away with; destroy, ruin, squander

pereō, -īre, -iī (-īvī), -itūrus: pass away, come to nothing, vanish, disappear, perish, be desperately in love with

perferō, -ferre, -tulī, -lātus: bear through, bring home

perfundō, -ere, -fūndī, perfūsus: soak, steep in, fill with

perlegō, -ere, -lēgī, -lēctus: examine thoroughly, scan, survey

pernīciter, *adv.:* nimbly, swiftly

pernīx, -īcis, *adj.:* persistent, persevering

pernumerō, -āre, -āvī, -ātus: count out, reckon up

perpetuus, -a, -um, *adj.:* continuous, unbroken, constant, perpetual

persequor, persequī, persecūtus sum: pursue, follow after with hostile intent, catch up with

pervigilō, -āre, -āvī, -ātus: watch all night, keep watch, remain awake

petō, -ere, -īvī (-iī, *perf.,* petit), petītus: seek, aim at, repair, strive for, go after

pharetra, -ae, *f.:* quiver, container filled with arrows

pharetrātus, -a, -um, *adj.:* wearing a quiver, quivered

Phoebus, -ī, *m.:* Apollo

Pīerius, -a, -um, *adj.:* Pierian, of Pieria (*in Macedonia*)

piger, pigra, pigrum: inactive, slow, inert

pīnguis, -e, *adj.:* fat

placeō, -ēre, -cuī, -ītus: be pleasing, please, be agreeable

plēbēs, plebēī, *f.:* common person, plebeian

plēnus, -a, -um, *adj.:* full

plōrō, -āre, -āvī, -ātus: weep or mourn aloud, bewail, weep over

plūrēs, -a, *(comp. adj. from* **multus**): more

plūrimum, *adv.:* very much, most, especially, for the most part

polluō, -ere, -uī, -ūtus: soil, defile, stain, foul, pollute

pondus, -eris, *n.:* a weight

pōnō, ponere, posuī, positus: place, put

porrigo, porrigere, porrexi, porrectus: stretched or spread out, spread (oneself) out; offer

porrō, *adv.:* forward, onward, farther

porta, -ae, *f.:* gate, entrance, city-gate

portentum, -ī, *n.:* portent, omen; something unnatural

possum, posse, potuī, —: be able

posterus, -a, -um, *adj.:* next, following

posthāc, *adv.:* hereafter, afterwards

postquam, *conjunction:* after

potēns, potēntis, *adj.:* powerful, influential

potis (pote), *indeclinable adj.:* able, capable (*in comp.,* preferable *or* better)

prae, *adv.:* before, in front of, in advance of

praebeō, praebēre, praebuī, praebitus: offer, hold out, present, provide

praedor, -ārī, -ātus sum, *deponent verb:* take booty, plunder

praesēns, -entis, *adj.:* at hand, in sight, present

praetereō, -īre, -iī, -itus: go by, pass by, pass, go past

precor, -ārī, -ātus sum, *deponent verb:* ask, beg, supplicate

prex, precis, *f.:* prayer, good wishes, curse

prīmus, -a, -um, *adj.:* first, foremost (*with* **digitum,** finger-tip)

prīscus, -a, -um, *adj.:* ancient, antique, old-fashioned, "good old days", former, previous

probō, -āre, -āvī, -ātus: approve, esteem well

procus, -ī, *m.:* suitor

prōficiō, -ere, -fēcī, -fectus: make headway, advance, make progress

prōnus, -a, -um, *adj.:* bent over, turned forward, inclined

prōpōnō, -ere, -posuī, -positus: put forth, set forth, lay out, expose, place before, display

proprius, -a, -um, *adj.:* one's own

prōsum, prōdesse, prōfuī, (*fut. inf.* **prōfore**): be useful, do good, benefit, profit

protervus, -a, -um: bold, impudent

prōtinus, *adv.:* directly, immediately

-pte, enclitic: self, own (*added to the abl. of possessive pronoun to emphasize inward possession*)

pūbēs, pubis, *f.:* men, the adult male population; puberty

pudendus, -a, -um, *adj.:* shameful, disgraceful

pudor, pudōris, *m.:* shame, dishonor

pūgna, -ae, *f.:* fight, battle, combat, action, engagement

pulcher, -chra, -chrum, *adj.:* beautiful, fair, handsome

pullus, -a, -um, *adj.:* dark, sad

pūmex, pumicis, *m.:* pumice stone, porous stone

purpureus, -a, -um, *adj.:* purple (*as in blushing*); beautiful

pūrus, -a, -um, *adj.:* pure, clean, unadorned, clear

putō, -āre, -āvī, -ātus: think, settle, suppose, clear up, estimate

Q

quaerō, -ere, -sīvī, -sītus: seek, look for, ask for, inquire

quālis, -e, *pronom. adj.:* of such a kind

quamvis, *adv. and conjunction:* as much as you please; however, although

quantuluscumque, -lacumque, -lumcumque, *adj.:* however small or insignificant

quatiō, quatere, —, quassus: shake, scatter, strike

queror, -ī, questus sum, *deponent verb:* lament, bewail, express grief

questus, -ūs, *m.:* complaint

quīcumque, quaecumque, quodcumque, *pronoun:* whoever, whatever, whosoever, whatsoever

quīn, *conjunction:* why not, wherefore not,

quisquis, quidquid, *pronoun and adj.:* whoever, whatever

quondam, *adv.:* at some time, at one time, once, heretofore

quotiēns, *adv.:* how often, whenever

R

radix, -īcis, *f.:* a root, a radish; foot, foundation, lower part

rādō, -ere, -sī, -sus: rub, smooth over; inscribe

rapidus, -a, -um, *adj.:* seizing, fierce, tearing away

raptō, -āre, -āvī, -ātus: ravage, drag off violently

raucus, -a, -um, *adj.:* hoarse

recreō, -āre, -āvī, -ātus: recreate, restore, revive

rēctus, -a, -um, *adj.:* straight, upright, direct

redeō, -īre, -iī, -itus: go back, turn back, return, turn around

redimiō, -īre, -iī, -ītus: encircle, gird

reflectō, -ere, -flexi, -flexus: bend back, turn backwards, turn about, turn away

regō, regere, rēxī, rēctus: guide, direct, govern, rule

rēiciō, reicere, rēiēci, reiectus: throw back, throw behind, throw away, reject, treat with scorn

religō, - āre, -āvī, -ātus: tie out of the way, bind back

remūgiō, remugīre, īvī, ītus: resound, reply

renovō, -āre, -āvī, -ātus: renew, restore

reperiō, -īre, repperī (reperī), repertus: find again, find, meet with, find out, discover

repertor, -ōris, *m.:* a discoverer, inventor, author

requīrō, -ere, -sīvī, -sītus: seek again, look after, search for

resecō, resecāre, resecuī, resectus: cut back, restrain, cut short

restitō, -āre, —, —: linger, loiter, wait behind

resurgō, -surgere, -surrēxī, -surrēctus: rise again, revive

retrō, *adv.:* backwards, back again, conversely

revertor, -ī, -versus sum, *deponent verb:* turn back, turn about, come back, return

rēx, rēgis, *m.:* a ruler, king, absolute monarch, royalty

rīdeō, rīdēre, rīsī, rīsus: laugh, smile

rigidus, -a, -um, *adj.:* stiff, unbending, inflexible

rōdō, -ere, -sī, -sus: gnaw, eat away at

rogō, -āre, -āvī, -ātus: ask, question, interrogate

rota, -ae, *f.:* wheel

rotō, -āre, -āvī, -ātus: roll around, whirl

rubeō, -ēre, —, —: be red

rubus, -ī, *m.:* bramble, thorn bush

rumor, -ōris, *m.:* a rustle, murmur, vague sound; *fig.* rumor, report, hearsay

S

sacer, -cra, -crum, *adj.:* dedicated, sacred, consecrated

saeviō, saevīre, saevīi, saevītus: rage, take violent action

saevus, -a, -um, *adj.:* savage, raging, ferocious

sāl, salis, *m.:* salt; *fig.* wit, acuteness, good sense

sānctus, -a, -um, *adj.:* sacred

sanguinulentus, -a, -um, *adj.:* bloody, covered in blood

sapiō, sapere, sapīvī, —: be wise, show good sense

satis, *indeclinable adj.:* sufficient, enough, ample

satus, -a, -um, *adj.:* spring from, native to

saucius, -a, -um, *adj.:* wounded, stricken, afflicted

scelestus, -a, -um, *adj.:* impious, wicked, accursed, wretched

scelus, sceleris, *n.:* wickedness, crime

sciō, -īre, -īvī, -ītus: know, understand, perceive, be skilled in

sēcrētus, -a, -um, *adj.:* severed, separated, separate, apart

sector, -ārī, -ātus sum, *deponent verb:* follow eagerly, run after, attend

secūres, -is, (-im *or* **-em** *acc.*)**,** *f.:* axe, hatchet, battle-axe

sedeō, -ēre, sēdī, sessus: sit

sēdulus, -a, -um, *adj.:* persistent, diligent

sēgnis, -e, *adj.:* slow, slack

semel, *adv.:* once, a single time

semper, *adv.:* ever, always, continually

senectūs, -ūtis, *f.:* old age, extreme age

senēscō, -ere, -nuī, —: grow old, grow hoary, become aged

senex, senis, *adj.:* old, aged

sensus, -ūs, *m.:* a perceiving, observation

sentiō, -īre, sēnsī, sēnsus: feel, discern by sense, perceive

sepulcrum, -ī, *n.:* burial-place, tomb, grave, sepulcher

sequor, sequī, secūtus sum, *deponent verb:* follow, pursue, go after

serviō, -īre, -īvī, -ītus: be a servant, be enslaved, serve

servus, -a, -um, *adj.:* having slave status, slavish, servile

sevērus, -a, -um, *adj.:* grave, serious, strict, stern, severe

seu(sive), *correlative:* whether, or if

sīc, *conjunction:* so, thus, in this way

sīdus, -eris, *n.:* a group of stars, constellation, the weather, the heavens

sīgnum, -ī, *n.:* sign, standard, mark, indication

silex, silicis, *m. and f.:* stone, hard stone, flint

silva, -ae , *f.:* woods

similis, -e, *adj.:* like, similar to

simplex, simplicis, *adj.:* simple, plain

simul, *adv.:* at the same time, together, at once

simulō, -āre, -āvī, -ātus: imitate, simulate, copy

sine, *prep. + abl.:* without

sinus, -ūs, *m.:* curve, bent surface; fold, hollow, coil

situs, -ūs, *m.:* neglect

sōbrius, -a, -um, *adj.:* sober, careful, aware

sodālis, -is, *m.:* companion

sōl, sōlis, *m.:* the sun

sōlāciolum, -ī, *n., diminutive:* a little comfort, a small solace

sōleō, -ēre, —, -itus: be accustomed to, use, be wont

sollemnis, -e, *adj.:* yearly, annual; solemn, religious, festive

sōlus, -a, -um (sōlīus *gen.;* **sōlī** *dat.*)**,** *adj.:* alone, solitary, lonely

solvō, -ere, solvī, solūtus: loosen, unbind, unfasten

somniō, -āre, -āvī, -ātus: dream, sleep

somnus, -ī, *m.:* sleep

sonitus, -ūs, *m.:* a noise, sound

sōpiō, -īre, -īvī, -ītus: stun, make unconscious, put to sleep

sopōrātus, -a, -um, *adj.:* asleep, stupefied

sordidus, -a, -um, *adj.:* dirty, shabby

sors, sortis, *f.:* lot, chance, fate, destiny

spargō, spargere, sparsī, sparsus: scatter, pour out, sprinkle

spatium, spatiī, *n.:* space *(of time)*

speculātor, -ōris, *m.:* scout, spy, explorer

spēs, speī, *f.:* hope, expectation, anticipation

spīculum, -ī, *n., diminutive:* arrow, point, sting

spurcō, -āre, -āvī, -ātus: defile

sternuō, -ere, -uī, —: sneeze, sputter, crackle

strepitus, -ūs, *m.:* noise, clash, clatter

strix, -igis, *f.:* screech-owl

suāvior, -ārī, -ātus sum, *deponent verb:* kiss

sublīmis, -e, *adj.:* raised, lifted

summus, -a, -um, *adj.:* uppermost, highest, topmost

sūmptus, -ūs, *m.:* expense, cost (generally high)

superbia, -ae, *f.:* pride, inflated self esteem, disdain

superō, -āre, -āvī, -ātus: go over, rise above, overtop, surmount, vanquish

superstes, -itis, *adj.:* outliving, surviving, standing over

supplex, supplicis, *adj.:* a suppliant, one making a humble request

sūra, -ae, *f.:* calf *(of the leg)*

surgō, -ere, surrēxī, surrēctus: rise, stand up, arise, get up

surripiō (subripiō), -ere, -ripuī, -reptus: snatch away, take secretly, withdraw, steal

suspendō, suspendere, suspendī, suspensus: hang up, prop up; leave undecided

suspicor, suspicārī, suspicātus sum, *deponent verb:* suspect, suppose

T

tabella, -ae, *f., diminutive:* tables, writing surface *(used especially for the composition of poetry)*

tabula, -ae, *f.:* a board or plank, writing tablet

taceō, -ēre, -cuī, -citus: be silent, not speak, say nothing, hold one's peace

tālis, -e, *adj.:* such, of such a kind, such like

tamen, *adv.:* however, nevertheless, yet

tandem, *adv.:* at last, at length, finally

tangō, tangere, tetigī, tāctus: touch, reach, strike, border on

tantum, *adv.:* so much, so greatly, to such a degree, so far so long

tēctum, -ī, *n.:* house, roof, shelter

tegō, -ere, tēxī, tēctus: cover, cover over

tellūs, tellūris, *f.:* land

temerē, *adv.:* by chance, by accident, casually

temperō, -āre, -āvī, -ātus: set bounds, exercise restraint, control oneself

tempestīvus, -a, -um, *adj.:* seasonable, mature

temptō, -āre, -āvī, -ātus: try, attempt, tamper with

teneō, -ēre, tenuī, tentus: hold, keep, have, grasp, hold fast

tener, -era, erum, *adj.:* tender, soft

tenuis, -e, *adj.:* drawn out, meager, slim, thin

teres, teretis, *adj.:* round, smooth, elegant

terminus, -ī, *m.:* boundary

terra, -ae, *f.:* earth, ground, land

terrēnus, -a, -um, *adj.,* terrestrial, belonging to the earth, mortal, earth-bound

terreō, terrēre, terruī, territus: frighten, terrify

tertius, -a, -um, *ordinal numeral adj.:* third

Thrācius, -a, -um, *adj.:* of Thrace *(a region north of Greece associated with Bacchus)*

Thrāx, -ācis, *adj.:* Thracian

thyrsus, -ī, *m.:* a staff *(carried by Dionysus)*

tigris, tigridis, (tigrim *acc.;* **tigrī** *abl.*),** *f.:* tiger

tingō (tinguō), tingere, tinxī, tīnctus: wet, stain, tint, dye

tintinō, -āre, -āvī, -ātus: ring, jingle, tingle

tollō, -ere, sustulī, sublātus: lift, take up, raise, elevate, exalt, remove, destroy

torreō, -ēre, torruī, tostus: dry up, parch, roast, bake, scorch

trādō, tradere, tradidī, traditus: hand over

tremō, tremere, tremuī, —: tremble, shake

trepidō, -āre, -āvī, -ātus: be agitated about, tremble; *with an infinitive,* be in a hurry

tribuō, tribuere, tribuī, tribūtus: assign, grant, allocate

trīstis, -e, *adj.:* sad, sorrowful

triumphus, -ī, *m.:* triumphal procession *(granted to a commander after a great victory)*

trivium, -ī, *n.:* crossroads

tueō, -ēre, —, —: defend, guard, care for, maintain (also **tueor, ērī,** *deponent verb*)

turma, -ae, *f.:* squadron of cavalry

turpis, -e, *adj.:* ugly, repulsive, unseemly, foul

Tyrrhēnus, -a, -um, *adj.:* Etruscan, Etrurian, Tuscan

U

ulcerōsus, -a, -um, *adj.:* full of sores, wounded

ulmus, -ī, *f.:* an elm tree

ūltimus, -a, -um, *adj.:* last, greatest

ūltrā, *prep. + acc.:* beyond, farther than

umquam, *adv.:* at any time, ever

ūndēnī, -ae, -a *(pl. only), adj.:* eleven each, eleven

unguis, -is, *m.:* a nail *(of the toe or finger)*

urbs, urbis, *f.:* a walled town, city

urgeō (urgueō), urgēre, ursī, —: push, press upon, embrace

ūrō, -ere, ussī, ūstus: burn, burn up, inflame with desire

ut (utī): how, as *(interrogative);* in order that, as, so that *(with subjunctive)*

ūtor, -ī, ūsus sum: *deponent verb:* use, profit from

ūva, -ae, *f.:* a grape, berry of the vine

ūvidus, -a, -um, *adj.:* wet

V

vacuus, -a, -um, *adj.:* free, available, empty, without; worthless

vadimōnium, -ī, *n.:* bail-bond, security

vae, *interjection:* alas!, ah!

vagor, vagārī, vagātus sum, *deponent verb:* wander

vānus, -a, -um, *adj.:* empty, useless

vārus, -a, -um, *adj.:* crooked, bent, turned away

vātēs, -is, *m. and f.:* prophet, seer, bard

vēctis, -is, *m.:* a lever, crowbar, instrument used for prying

vellō, -ere, vellī, vulsus: pluck, pull, tear out

vēna, -ae, *f.:* streak, vein

venēnātus, -a, -um, *adj.:* filled with poison, poisonous

ventilō, -āre, -āvī, -ātus: kindle, fan, toss in the air

ventitō, -āre, -āvī, —: come often, keep coming, resort

ventus, -ī, *m.:* wind, air

Venus, Veneris, *f.:* Venus

venus, -eris, *f.:* loveliness, attractiveness, grace, elegance

venustās, -ātis, *f.:* charm, elegance, beauty, loveliness

vēr, vēris, *n.:* spring

verbēna, -ae, *f.:* sacred boughs, flowers

vērē, *adv.:* truly, really

verrō, -ere, verrī, versus: sweep, set sail, brush, scour

vertex (vortex), vertices, *m.:* at the top of, the summit, that which turns

vēsānus, -a, -um, *adj.:* unsound of mind, insane, mad

vestīmentum, -ī, *n.:* clothing, a garment

vetus, -eris, *adj.:* old, aged, advanced in years

victor, victōris, *m.:* conqueror

victōria, -ae, *f.:* victory

victrīx, -icis, *adj.:* reporting a victory, victorious

viden (vidēsne = vides + ne): do you see that?

vidua, -ae, *f.:* unmarried woman, widow

vigeō, vigēre: flourish, thrive

vīlis, -e, *adj.:* of small price, cheap

vinciō, vincīre, vinxī, vinctus: bend around, wrap around, surround

vincō, -ere, vīcī, vīctus: conquer, overcome, defeat

vinculum, -ī, *n.:* rope, binding, chain

vīnum, -ī, *n.:* wine

viola, -ae, *f., noun and adj.:* the color violet; (*as an adj.,* violet)

vir, virī, *m.:* man, husband

virginitās, -ātis, *f.:* maidenhood, virginity

virgō, virginis, *f.:* girl, maiden

viridis, -e, *adj.:* green

vīs (vim *acc.,* **vī** *abl.,* **virēs** *pl.*),** *f.:* strength, force, power; a large quantity; power or influence

vīta, -ae, *f.:* life

vītis, -is, *f.:* grapevine

vītō, -āre, -āvī, -ātus: avoid, shun

vīvō, -ere, vīxī, vīctus: live, be alive, have life, live well

vix, *adv.:* with difficulty, hardly, scarcely, barely

volō, velle, voluī, —: wish, want, propose, be minded

volō, -āre, -āvī, -ātus: fly

voltur, -uris, *m.:* vulture

volturius, -ī, *m.:* a vulture-like bird, bird of prey, vulture

vorō, -āre, -āvī, -ātus: swallow whole, eat greedily, devour

vōtivus, -a, -um, *adj.:* votive, promised, volved

vulgus, -ī, *n. and m.:* the general public, the masses

vultus (voltus), -ūs, *m.:* face, expression, aspect

Z

zōna, -ae, *f.:* a woman's girdle, belt, zone

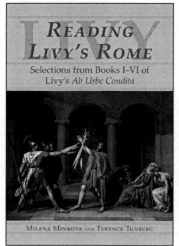

READING
LIVY'S ROME
Selections from Books I–VI of
Livy's *Ab Urbe Condita*

MILENA MINKOVA AND TERENCE TUNBERG

READING LIVY'S ROME

Selections from Books I–VI of Livy's *Ab Urbe Condita*

Milena Minkova and Terence Tunberg

Student: xii + 276 pp., 6 b&w illus. (2005)
6" x 9" Paperback, ISBN 0-86516-550-5

Teacher: vi + 114 pp. (2005)
6" x 9" Paperback, ISBN 0-86516-600-5

EASE STUDENTS
INTO READING LIVY'S HISTORY

High-interest graded readings from Books I–VI of Livy's *Ab Urbe Condita:* Romulus and Remus, Cincinnatus, and more. Paraphrases with vocabulary stand opposite simplified and annotated Livian passages. Readings progress to authentic Livian passages, annotated but with fewer vocabulary aids. Appendix of authentic Livian passages for all simplified selections.

Features: • Simple Latin paraphrases for pre-reading • Extensive same-page glossaries • Inserts on features of Livy's language • English section titles for easy context • Graduated Livian Latin passages • Graduated notes on syntax and grammar • Full vocabulary

Teacher's Guide Features: literal translation of the paraphrases

About the authors:
Milena Minkova has published widely on medieval Latin and Latin reference/composition. She holds a PhD in Classics from the University of Sofia, Bulgaria, and a PhD in Christian and Classical Studies from the Pontifical Salesian University, Rome. She currently holds a full-time position in the Department of Classical Languages at the University of Kentucky.

Terence Tunberg has published widely on medieval and neo-Latin and is founder of the electronic Latin journal *Retiarius.* He holds a PhD in Classics from the University of Toronto. He is an Associate Professor in the Department of Classical Languages and teaches in the Honors Program at the University of Kentucky.

BOLCHAZY-CARDUCCI PUBLISHERS, INC.
WWW.BOLCHAZY.COM